简明汉语语法

郭振华 著

A CONCISE CHINESE GRAMMAR

by
Guo Zhenhua

华语教学出版社
北京

SINOLINGUA
Beijing, China

gbd books
New Delhi, India

A Concise Chinese Grammar

First Indian Edition 2009

This special authorised low-priced Indian reprint is published by arrangement with Sinolingua, China for sale in the Indian Subcontinent

ISBN 978-81-88951-40-6

Published by
gbd books
I-2/16, Ansari Road, Daryaganj
New Delhi-110002, India
PH: 23260022; 41563695, 9810229648
E-mail: kaushalgoyal@yahoo.com
Website: www.goyalbookshop.com

Distributed by
General Book Depot
1691, Nai Sarak, Delhi - 110006
Ph.: 23263695; 23250635; 9312286851
Email: generalbookdepot@yahoo.com
Website: www.generalbooks.com

Printed at
Radha Press
2465, Main Road, Kailash Nagar, Delhi-110031
radha.press@yahoo.co.in

Foreword

This book is written as a grammar text for foreign students who have studied Chinese for two or more years and are at intermediate level in the Chinese language. It provides a basic outline of Chinese grammar for the students, a general description of the principles and unique features of Chinese grammar, so that the students can have an overall understanding of the grammar.

The book consists of nine chapters including functional analysis, comparison of words, syntactic structure and sentence types along with practice exercises. The author's goal in writing has been to provide simple and clear discriptions, emphasizing important points and highlighting discriminations. In using the book, the teacher can make use of the actual questions students have, emphasize the practice on difficult points and analysis of incorrect sentences. Through much practice, it is possible to achieve the goal of an accurate grasp and use of the Chinese language.

Professor Thelmas Chow(U.S.A.)translated the book into English. Here I want to express my appreciation for him. Acknowledgements are also extended to Mr Shi Chunhong and Mr Jia Yinhuai who have made great efforts for the publishing of this book.

The Author

May, 1999

前　言

本书是为具有中等汉语水平的外国学生编写的汉语语法教材,适合于学过两年以上汉语的外国学生使用。

本书为学习者提供了汉语语法的基本轮廓,概括地叙述了汉语语法的一般规则和特点,使学习汉语的外国学生对汉语语法有一个系统全面的了解。

全书共分九章,对词、句法结构和句子分别进行了功能分析和比较,并附有练习。

在编写过程中,作者力求叙述简明扼要,抓住重点,突出区别。使用时,教师可结合学生学习汉语中的实际问题进行教学,突出难点练习和病句分析,通过大量的练习来达到正确掌握和运用汉语的目的。

美国郭欣培教授翻译了全书,谨此致谢。

施春宏、贾寅淮二位同志为此书出版付出了大量心血,在此一并致谢。

作者

1999 年 5 月

目　　录
Table of Contents

第一章　词　　类
Chapter One　Word Classes

第一节　字和语素
Characters and Morphemes

中国传统的用语是"字"和"句"，学习文化从认字开始，一般人便以为句子是由字组成的，这就混淆了字和词的界限。

The traditional terms used in China are "character"(字) and "sentence"(句). Learning character is where the study of the culture begins. Most people believe that sentences are formed with characters, but this obscures the boundary between character and word.

字和词不是一个东西。字是书面上的方块字，是书写符号，又是读音单位。有的字有意义，有的字没有意义。

Characters and words are two different things. Characters are the square written symbols. They are also units of pronunciation. Some characters have meaning, others do not.

有意义的如 Examples of those with meaning:

人　牛　书　我　去　好

无意义的如 Examples of those without meaning:

垃　圾　葡　萄　玻　璃

一个字可以是一个词,一个词可以是几个字。例如:

A character can be a word, a word could be several characters. For example:

山　天　美　来　在　了　啊

行李　巧克力　奥林匹克　马克思主义

中华人民共和国

现在来看看字和语素的关系。汉语里的语素,单音节的多,所以人们常常以为语素就是字,其实,语素和字也不是一个东西。下面,我们看看语素的大小、异同以及与汉字的对应关系。

In Chinese, most morphemes are monosyllabic, so people often believe that morphemes are characters when in fact, morphemes and characters are not one and the same. Below we will analyze the size, similarities of morphemes, and their relationships with Chinese characters.

1. 一个汉字可以代表几个语素。

One character can represent several different morphemes.

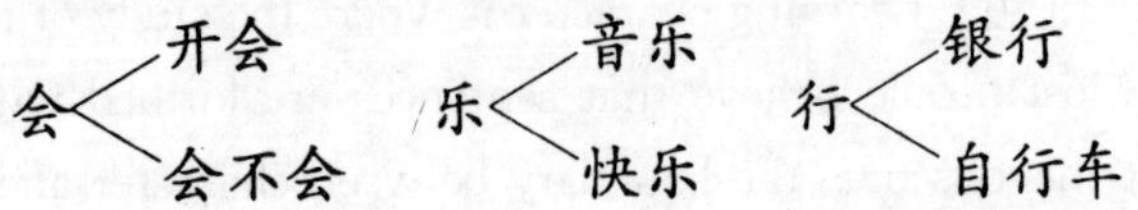

2. 一个汉字在某种场合是语素,在另一种场合不是语素。

The same character may be a morpheme in one context but not in another.

沙子　发展　马车　达到

巧遇　克服　力量

带点的字都是语素。 All the dotted characters are morphemes.

沙发　马达　巧克力

带点的每个字都不是语素。 None of the dotted characters are

morphemes.

3. 无意义的汉字不是语素。例如：

Characters without meaning are not morphemes. For example:

玫　瑰　琵　琶　徘　徊　朦　胧

在“菠菜、啤酒、冰淇淋”等词中，“菠、啤、淇淋”都无意义，但“菜、酒、冰”有意义，都是语素，在这种情况下，我们也将“菠、啤、淇淋”看成语素。

字虽然不等于语素，但对于认识分析语素是有帮助的。

菠，啤，淇淋 have no meaning, but 菜，酒，冰 have meanings and are morphemes. In this case, we consider 菠，啤，淇淋 as morphemes. Although characters are not morphemes, they are important in the analysis of the morphemes.

第二节　语素和词
Morphemes and Words

我们分析句子结构时，只分析到词。可见，句法是以词为单位的，不是以语素为单位的。但是，我们要认识什么是词，又不能不首先了解什么是语素，因为词是由语素构成的。

When we analyze sentence structure we analyze only to the word level. It is clear that in syntax the unit is word and not morpheme. However, if we want to understand words, it is not possible for us to do so without first understanding what a morpheme is since words are constructed by morphemes.

语素是最小的有意义的语言成分。词是语言中最小的能独立运用的有意义的语言单位。

语素是构成词的建筑材料,词是构成句子的建筑材料。

语素的特点在于意义上不能再分割,词的特点在于能独立运用。

语素和词的区别在于是否能单用。例如:

Morphemes are the smallest meaningful components of language. Words are the smallest meaningful units of language which can be used independently. Morphemes are the building material for words, and words are the building material for sentences. The unique feature of morphemes is that there can be no further break down for meaning; the unique feature of words is that they can be used independently. The difference between morphemes and words is the ability to be used alone. For examples:

	语素 Morpheme	词 Word
大	1	1
衣	1	
飞	1	1
机	1	
我	1	1
们	1	
葡萄	1	1
大衣	2	1
飞机	2	1

我们　　2　　1

上面例子中的“大、飞、我”能单独构成词,“衣、机、们”不能单独构成词。

In the examples above 大,飞,我 can bc used alone as words, 衣,机,们 cannot be used as words alone.

不能单独构成词的语素不是词(如:衣、机、们),能单独构成词的语素有时是词,有时不是词(如:大、飞、我)。

Morphemes which cannot form words alone are not words(e.g. 衣,机,们). Morphemes which can form words alone may sometimes be words and sometimes not (e.g. 大,飞,我).

一个语素可以是一个词,还可以是一个句子。例如:

A morpheme may be a word or it may be a sentence. For example:

“谁?”　“我。”

两个语素组合起来可能是词,也可能是词组。例如:

Two morphemes together may be a word or a word group. For example:

吃饭:①吃米饭(词组 phrase)
　　　②进餐(词 word)
大车:①大的车(词组 phrase)
　　　②马车(词 word)

一般来说,语法研究的范围是从语素到句子:

In general, the realm of grammatical analysis is from morpheme to sentence.

语素、词 } 词法(研究组词的规则)
词组、句子 } 句法(研究造句的规则)
} 语法

morphemes words	morphology	(the study of rules of word formation)	grammar
word groups sentences	syntax	(the study of rules of sentence formation)	

由一个语素构成的词叫单纯词，由两个以上的语素构成的词叫合成词。

A word made up of one morpheme is called a simple word. A word composed of two or more morphemes is called a compound word.

单纯词如 Examples of simple word are:

大　飞　我　牛　树　葡萄

合成词如 Examples of compound word are:

大衣　飞机　我们　水牛　茶树

根据成词不成词，语素可分为自由语素和黏着语素。自由语素能单独成词，黏着语素不能单独成词。

Based on whether or not a morpheme can be a word, morphemes can be divided into free morphemes and bound morphemes. Free morphemes can become independent words, while bound morphemes cannot.

由自由语素组成的词如：

Examples of words composed of free morphemes are:

车头　海味　空气　电话　话剧　电影

国家　西瓜　火车　白菜　好看　雨伞

由黏着语素组成的词如：

Examples of words composed of bound morphemes are:

今年　儿女　武器　舒服　研究　聪明

由自由语素和黏着语素合成的词如：

Examples of words composed of free and bound morphemes are:

年轻　京剧　学校　声音　牙膏　房间

美丽　城市　雨衣　飞机　附近　秋天

外来词中有的是单纯词，如：

Among loan words some are simple words, such as:

葡萄　玻璃　柠檬　罗汉　和尚　菩萨

马达　瓦斯　鸦片　雪茄　咖啡　雷达

幽默　摩登　沙发　逻辑　马克　拷贝

模特儿　法西斯　尼古丁　俱乐部

奥林匹克　阿司匹林　歇斯底里　可口可乐

有的是合成词，如：

Some are compound words, such as:

卡车　卡片　酒吧　啤酒　吉普车

可可糖　茉莉花　冰淇淋　乒乓球

爵士乐　迪斯科舞　白兰地酒　高尔夫球

练　　习

一、指出下列语言单位哪些是语素，哪些是词：

山	河	国	丽	居
术	梦	然	垃	长江
卡车	钱包	世界	电脑	球迷
沙龙	色拉	扑克	巧克力	三明治
尼古丁	芭蕾舞	乒乓球	北半球	北京大学

二、下面所举的都是词组,你能说出每个词组中包含几个语素、几个词吗?

看电影	非常好看
骑摩托车	走不了
钥匙丢了	五香瓜子
电脑公司	他会弹吉它

三、请指出哪些是词,哪些是词组:

新闻( )	领带( )	好说( )
电扇( )	高楼( )	梦想( )
管家( )	京剧( )	三鲜汤( )
玫瑰花( )	鸡尾酒( )	麦克风( )
北京市( )	留学生( )	麻辣豆腐( )
高尔夫球( )	明信片( )	借书证( )
售货员( )	天津包子( )	公共汽车( )
百科全书( )	超级市场( )	十字路口( )
中秋节( )	星期天( )	代表团( )
国内外( )	电影明星( )	世界冠军( )

第三节　划分词类的依据
The Basis for Designating Word Classes

词是构成句子的建筑材料,但是并不是所有的词在造句中的作用都是一样的。不同的词在造句中的功能是不相同的,这就要对词进行分类。下面举例看看词在句法结构中的作用:

Words are the building materials for constructing sentences, but words are not all used in the same way in the construction of sentences. Different words have different functions, so they are classified into different classes. The following examples illustrate the functions of words in syntactical construction.

A 组	B 组
Group A	Group B
新书	买书
厚书	借书
好书	看书

A 组里,"新书" "厚书" "好书"之间在结构关系上是相同的,但词汇意义不同,它们的不同是因为成分不同。

B 组里,"买书" "借书" "看书"之间在结构关系上是相同的,但词汇意义不同,它们的不同也是因为成分不同。

In Group A, 新书,厚书,好书 are the same in terms of structural relationships, but they are not the same in lexical meaning; the difference is in the components. In Group B, 买书,借书,看书 are the same in terms of structural relationships, but not the same in lexical meaning; the difference again is in the components.

A 组和 B 组之间,除了词汇意义不同以外,结构关系也不同,它们的不同是因为语法功能不同。

However, between Group A and Group B, in addition to a difference in lexical meaning, there is also a difference in structural relationships, the difference being one of grammatical function.

我们再看另外一组例子:

Here are some other examples:

甲组	乙组	丙组
Group One	Group Two	Group Three
看	书	刚
唱	歌	不
听	音乐	也
骑	马	常

这三组词之间的结构关系是:

The structural relationships among the three groups are as follows:

甲+乙:看书　　（述宾　verb object）
甲+丙:×
乙+甲:书看(了)（主谓　subject predicate）
乙+丙:×
丙+甲:刚看　　（偏正　endocentric construction）
丙+乙:×

由此可见:

甲组:能作谓语　　动词　verbs
乙组:能作主语、宾语　　名词　nouns
丙组:只能作状语　　副词　adverbs

Thus, Group One　may be predicates
Group Two　may be subjects or objects
Group Three　may be adverbials

从这两组例子中,我们可以看出:词在造句中的作用是不同的,这种不同的作用是由词的不同语法功能造成的。

From these two sets of examples, we can see that words are used in different ways in the creation of sentences. This difference in usage is due to a difference in grammatical function.

一个词的语法功能指的是这个词在句法结构里所能占据的语法位置。

The grammatical function of a word refers to the grammar slots it can fill in the syntactical structure.

同类的词必须有相同的语法功能。说功能相同并不是完全相同。例如,作谓语的不仅是动词,还有形容词等。

下面我们举例说明这一点。例如:

Words in the same class function the same way grammatically. But to say the functions are the same is not to say that they are identical. For example, verbs are not the only class which can serve as predicates, adjectives may also. This point is illustrated below. For example:

	爱惜	汽车	希望
有 +	−	+	+
数量 +	−	+	+
很多 +	−	+	+
不 +	+	−	+
作谓语	+	−	+
	动词	名词	名动词

旧:
1. 前加“很”
2. 后加“的”
3. 后加“了”
4. 作谓语
5. 作定语

买:
1. 带宾语
2. 前加“刚”“不”
3. 后加“的”
4. 后加“了”“过”
5. 作谓语

上面两组例子分别检验了名词和动词、动词和形容词的区别性特征。

The two groups of examples above examine the differentiating characteristics of nouns and verbs and of verbs and adjectives.

根据词的语法功能来对词进行分类是完全可以做到的。

也就是说，词类是词的语法分类。这个定义很概括，也很含混。它可能被理解为包括意义和功能两方面。

在词类划分的标准问题上，语法学家通常主要从词的意义、功能和形态三个方面来确定划分的标准。

我们先来看词的意义。

It is entirely possible to classify words based on how they function grammatically. Word classes are the grammar classes of words. This definition is very general and quite ambiguous and can be understood as including both meaning and function. As to the standard of word classification, grammarians usually define standards by meaning, function, and form of words. First, let's discuss the meaning of words.

名词：表示事物的名称。

Nouns: Express the name of something.

动词：表示动作或行为。

Verbs: Express action or behavior.

形容词：表示事物的性质或状态。

Adjectives: Express the nature or state of something.

实际上，表示同类概念的词，其语法性质不一定相同。例如：

In fact, words which express similar concepts do not necessarily have the same grammatical features. For example:

战争（名词 noun）
战斗（动词 verb） } 意义相同 similar meaning

红（形容词 adjective）
红色（名词 noun） } 意义相同 similar meaning

突然（形容词 adjective）
忽然（副词 adverb） } 意义相同 similar meaning

如果只从意义上看是不容易区分的，如果从功能上看就十分清楚。例如："突然"可以用来作谓语、宾语、补语，而"忽然"只能用来作状语。

Considering only from the angle of meaning, it is difficult to differentiate; when taking function into account, it is quite clear. For example, 突然 can be used as a predicate, an object, or a complement while 忽然 can be used only as an adverbial.

这件事很突然。

我感到突然。

他来得很突然。

他 忽然 / 突然 病了。

可见，根据词义来划分词类是很困难的。

Therefore it is very difficult to classify words by their meaning.

我们再看词的形态。

按词的形态变化来划分词类，我们只能举其他语言的例子。如在英语中，名词 + s 表示复数；形容词 + er、est 表示比较级、最高级；动词 + ed 表示过去时。

Now let us look at the issue of form. To classify words by form, we can only use examples form other languages, in English for example: Noun + s shows plurality; adjective + er, est shows comparative or superlative degree; verb + ed shows past tense.

car, tree, book } + s

big, old, long } + er / + est

work, collect, look } + ed

形态标志和形态变化是语法功能的一种表现形式。按形态分类实际上也是按语法功能给词分类。由于汉语缺少形态标志，给词分类是困难的，只能根据语法功能划分词类。

Inflectional markings or changes in form are methods of indicating grammatical function. In fact, to differentiate word classes by form is the same as by grammatical function. Because Chinese lacks inflectional markings, classes can be differentiated only on the basis of function.

第四节　现代汉语词类概况
Survey of Word Classes in Modern Chinese

大致可以分为十二类：

In general, there are twelve classes:

名词(Nouns)： 人、马、树、花、水、学生、机器、历史、社会、精神、中国、情况、今天、下午、上边、中间

动词(Verbs)： 走、飞、写、是、有、想、爱、来、去、喜欢、改变、成为、同意、会

形容词(Adjectives)： 大、小、好、坏、高、低、甜、干净、美丽、认真、热闹、公共、有效、任何、唯一

数词(Numerals)： 一、二、三、四、五、六、十、半百、千、万、亿、两；第一、第二

量词(Measure words)： 个、件、本、张、斤、块、条、公斤、公尺、吨、次、架次、回、下、遍、阵、番

代词(Pronouns)： 我、你、他、我们、你们、他们、您、咱们、这、那、这么、那样、谁、什么、哪儿、哪个、几、多少

副词(Adverbs)： 很、太、也、只、又、再、还、就、更、不、才、马

上、偏偏、非常、已经、仍然、简直、难道

介词(Prepositions)： 把、被、为、替、给、比、向、从、对、对于、由于、为了、除了、按照、至于

连词(Conjunctions)： 和、跟、同、及、并且、而且、与、或者、不但、而且、于是、但是、虽然、即使、既然、只要、尽管、如果、不论、因为、所以、因此、否则、与其、不如、然而

助词(Auxiliaries)： 了、着、过；的、地、得、所、似的；吗、呢、吧、啊、呀、了

叹词(Interjections)： 啊、唉、哟、喂

象声词(Onomatopoeia)： 呼、啪、嘟、嗞、哗啦、咔嚓、叮当、乒乓、咕嘟

几点说明 Notes:

1. 名词、动词、形容词、数词、量词、代词统称为实词。实词有实在的意义，在句中的位置自由，属于开放性的。

副词、介词、连词、助词、叹词、象声词统称为虚词。虚词没有实在的意义，在句中的位置固定，属于封闭性的(即数量有限)。

Nouns, verbs, adjectives, numerals, measure words, and pronouns are called notional words. Notional words have definite meanings, are flexible in placement in the syntax, and belong to open types.

Adverbs, prepositions, conjunctions, auxiliaries, interjections, and onomatopoeia are called function words. Function words lack a definite meaning, their placement in syntax is fixed and they belong to closed types (limited in number).

2. 名词中包括时间词、方位词、处所词，动词中包括助动词，形容词中包括状态词和非谓形容词；助词中包括语气词。

Nouns include time words, position words, and location words. Verbs include auxiliary verbs. Adjectives include statives and non-predicative adjectives. Auxiliaries include tonal or mood words.

3. 叹词、象声词一般归入虚词，可是它们能单说，不同于其他类虚词。

Interjections and onomatopoeia are generally classed as function words, but they are unlike other function words in that they can be used independently.

词类总表 Chart of Word Classes

实词	名词	名词	工人 太阳 社会 战争
		时间词	今年 从前 现在 上午
		方位词	上 下 里 外 东南 中间
	数词	基数词	一 二 三 四……九 十 千 万
		序数词	第一 第二 第三 第四
	量词	名量词	个 件 张 把 条 块
		动量词	次 回 阵 趟 番 场
	代词	人称代词	我 你 他 我们 你们
		疑问代词	谁 什么 哪儿 哪个 几
		指示代词	这 这个 那 那里 这样
	动词	动词	看 听 想 喜欢 计划
		助动词	能 会 要 愿意 应该
	形容词	形容词	好 坏 香 美丽 伟大
		状态词	雪白 冰凉 火热 绿油油
		区别词	男 女 正 副 金 中式 慢性
虚词	副词		很 太 已经 非常 马上 终于
	介词		把 被 对 比 由于 按照
	连词		和 跟 同 与 或者 不但
	助词	结构助词	的 地 得 所
		时态助词	了 着 过
		语气助词	吗 吧 呢 的 了 啊
	象声词		呼 啪 嘟 哗啦 叮当
	叹词		啊 唉 哟 喂

第五节　名词、动词、形容词

Nouns, Verbs and Adjectives

一、名词　Nouns

意义:表示事物。既可指具体的事物,也可指抽象的事物。

Definition: identify things (concrete or abstract).

特点 Characteristics:

1. 可以受数量词修饰。例如:

May be qualified by measure words. Examples:

一本书　一支笔　一把钥匙

2. 不受副词修饰。例如:

Cannot be qualified by adverbs. Examples:

*不青年　*很友谊

3. 可以做主语、宾语、定语,不能作状语、补语,少数名词可以直接作谓语。例如:

May serve as subject, object, attributive, but not as adverbials or complements; a few nouns can serve alone as predicate. Examples:

今天星期二　　他北京人

十一国庆节　　那孩子黄头发

昨天阴天

分类 Categories:

1. 事物名词 Nouns which name things: 人、苹果、屋子、空气、

友谊、和平、对象

2. 专有名词 Proper nouns:北京、火星、黄河、王府井、鲁迅、红楼梦

3. 集合名词 Collective nouns:人民、人口、纸张、船只、车辆、马匹、花朵、房间

4. 时间名词 Time nouns:秋天、夜间、星期五、中秋节

5. 方位名词 Nouns of position:上、下、里、外、左、右、前、后、东、西、南、北、中、上边、里面、前头、西北、中间

二、动词 Verbs

意义:表示动作、行为、存在、变化或意愿。例如:

Definition: Express action, behavior, existence, change or will.

Examples:

走	看	笑	学习	参观
想	喜欢	怕	恨	同意
是	有	在	到	成为
能	会	要	应该	愿意

特点 Characteristics:

1. 能受副词"不"的修饰。

May be qualified by the adverb 不 .

2. 除少数表示心理活动的动词(如:想、爱、喜欢)外,不能受"很"的修饰。

Except for a few verbs which express mental activity(想,爱,喜欢),they may not be qualified by 很 .

3. 作谓语,后可跟"了、着、过"。

May be predicates,and followed by 了,着 and 过 .

4. 大多数动词能带宾语(如:看、写、寻找、修理),少数动词不能带宾语(如:咳嗽、合作、醒、休息、游行)。

Most verbs may take an object(看,写,寻找,修理).A few verbs cannot take objects(咳嗽,合作,醒,休息,游行).

5. 可以重叠。单音节按 AA 式重叠,双音节按 ABAB 式重叠。例如:

May be duplicated. The monosyllabic verbs are duplicated in the form of AA, while the disyllabic verbs in the form of ABAB. Examples:

写写　看看　讨论讨论　打听打听

分类　Categories:

1. 及物动词与不及物动词(根据能否带宾语分)

Transitive and intransitive verbs (based on whether or not they take an object)

及物动词　Transitive verbs:看、洗、拿、修、知道、支持、是、有

不及物动词　Intransitive verbs:休息、合作、帮忙、睡觉、游行、咳嗽

有的兼有及物不及物(带不带宾语意思不同),例如:

Transitive or Intransitive(The meaning is different depending on whether or not there is an object):

笑 { 他笑了 / 他笑你 }　　哭 { 他哭了 / 他哭他奶奶 }

死 { 他死了 / 他死了父亲 }　　丢 { 他丢了 / 他丢了手表 }

败 { 他败了 / 他败了对方 }　　摔 { 他摔了 / 他摔了一个杯子 }

2. 名动词　Nominal verbs

意义:具有名词和动词语法特征的词。例如:

Definition: Words which have the grammatical properties of both nouns and verbs. For example:

斗争　研究　计划　影响　工作　准备

批评　报告　记录　习惯　休息　宣传

确定条件　Ways to identify nominal verbs:

(1) 能出现在"有""进行""受到"之后。例如:

May be used after 有,进行,受到. For example:

有计划　进行研究　受到批评

(2) 能受名词的直接修饰。例如:

May be directly qualified by nouns. For example:

思想准备　工业计划　历史研究　政治影响

(3) 能直接修饰名词。例如:

May themselves directly qualify nouns. For example:

准备工作　休息时间　斗争历史

3. 助动词(能愿动词)　Auxiliary verbs(optative verbs)

意义:表示可能、意愿。例如:

Definition: Express possibility or intention. Examples:

能　会　要　可以　应该　必须

应当　愿意　值得　敢

确定条件　Ways to identify:

(1) 只能带动词宾语。例如:

Take only verbal objects:

能去　会说

(2) 能单说。如:

May be used alone:

可以　要

(3) 能放入“～不～”式中。例如:

May be used in ～不～ question form:

能不能来　应该不应该做

(4) 不能出现在动词“有”“作”之后。

May not be used after the verb 有 or 作 .

*有会　*作可以

(5) 不能重叠。

May not be duplicated.

(6) 不能带“了、着、过”。

May not be followed by 了,着 or 过 .

三、形容词 Adjectives

意义:表示事物的性质或状态。例如:

Definition: Express nature or condition of something. Examples:

红　好　高　大　新　快　甜　真

聪明　干净　漂亮　认真　正确

特点 Characteristics:

1. 大部分受副词修饰。否定用“不”。

The majority may be qualified by adverbs. May be negated with 不 .

2. 大部分可以重叠。方式是 AA 式、AABB 式。

The majority may be duplicated, the form being AA, AABB.

3. 能作谓语、定语,部分可以作状语。

May be predicates, attributives; some can be adverbials.

分类 Categories:

1. 性质形容词和状态形容词　Adjectives of characteristic and adjectives of condition

性质形容词有单音节的和双音节的。单音节的如：

Adjectives of characteristic can be divided into monosyllabic and disyllabic. Examples of monosyllabic are:

小　红　大　好　快　甜　美

双音节的如　Examples of disyllabic are:

干净　漂亮　仔细　正确　聪明

状态形容词主要指的是形容词重叠式。形容词重叠式是形容词的一种复杂形式。其构成方式如下：

Adjectives of condition mainly refer to the duplication of adjective. Duplication of adjectives is a complex form of adjectives. Following are the various ways of forming them:

单音节形容词重叠式是：

Duplication of monosyllablic adjectives:

红红的　大大的　圆圆的　高高的

轻轻地　快快地　好好地　满满地

还有一类是附加成分重叠：

Another type is the duplication of an added element:

红艳艳　冷清清　气乎乎　空洞洞

轻飘飘　干巴巴　血淋淋　孤零零

双音节形容词重叠式是：

Way of duplicating disyllabic adjectives:

干干净净的　高高兴兴的　随随便便的

规规矩矩的　和和气气的　马马虎虎的

还有一类是部分重叠：

Duplication of one part:

糊里糊涂的　慌里慌张的　古里古怪的

小里小气的　娇里娇气的　啰里啰嗦的

形容词重叠式表示某种感情色彩，它的语法意义跟它所在的语法位置有关。如“红红的”作定语或谓语时，在程度上比“红”要浅一些。例如：

Duplicated adjectives carry a certain emotional or mood tone. The grammatical meaning is related to the grammar slot it fills. When 红红的 is an attributive or a predicate it means something a little less in degree than 红 . For example:

红红的高粱酒。

她的脸红红的。

“轻轻地”作状语时，在程度上比“轻”要重一些。例如：

When 轻轻地 is an adverbial, it is a degree heavier than 轻. For example:

一百四十斤的杠铃他轻轻地一举就起来了。

大吊车轻轻地一抓就起来。

少数表示消极意义的形容词如“坏、破、脏、臭、穷、怪”等很少重叠，重叠之后，原来的意义有所减退，甚至可爱。例如：

A few adjectives with negative meanings such as 坏，破，脏，臭，穷 and 怪 are seldom duplicated. When they are, the original meaning is lessened to the extent that it could mean cute or likeable. For example:

那孩子脸蛋脏脏的。

他样子蠢蠢的。

2．区别词　Non-predicative adjectives

不具有形容词的特点而又像形容词的类。例如：

They do not have the same characteristics as adjectives, but are similar to the adjective class. For example:

男 女 正 副 金 单 双

西式 中式 新式 非正式 大型 微型

小型 慢性 烈性 急性 高等 上等

彩色 黑白 超级 中号 高速 万能

长期 短期 野生 专用 精装 特约

人造 天然 国产 民用 电动 国营 私营

半旧 正方 草绿 金黄 银白

有色 无名 任何

中华 公共 主要 中小

特点 Characteristics:

(1) 直接修饰名词。例如:

Directly qualify nouns:

男上衣 女教师 副部长

(2) 大部分加"的"。例如:

Most can be followed by 的:

唯一的 主要的 有色的

(3) 可放入"是……的"中。例如:

Can be used in the construction 是…的:

衣服是中号的 玩具是电动的

(4) 不能作主语宾语。例如:

Cannot be subjects or objects:

*男不男 *坐大型

(5) 不能作谓语。例如:

Cannot be predicates:

*飞机国产 *酒烈性

(6) 不受"很""不"修饰。例如：

Cannot be qualified by 很 or 不:

*很新式　*不人造(不高级)

上面六个特点,(1)(2)(3)很像形容词,可是(6)却不像形容词,(4)不同于名词,(5)不同于动词。

In the six points above, (1), (2) and (3) are like adjectives, but (6) is not at all like adjectives. Number (4) is unlike nouns, (5) unlike verbs.

我们说大部分形容词能受"很""不"的修饰,大部分可以重叠,能作谓语、定语、状语。

区别词不能受"很""不"修饰,不能重叠,不能作谓语、状语,可是能作定语,修饰限制中心语。

所以,我们把它归入形容词里,作为一个小类。意义上表示区别、分类。例如：

Most adjectives may take the qualifiers 很 and 不, and can be duplicated. Most can be predicates, attributives, and adverbials.

Non-predicative adjectives may not take the qualifiers 很 and 不, cannot be duplicated, cannot be predicates or adverbials but may be attributives, qualifying only head words. Therefore, we include them as a small class in the adjective category. They express distinction or difference as in the following examples:

男	正	单	西式	国营	彩色	大型
女	副	双	中式	私营	黑白	小型

长期	慢性	高级	天然	有限	正式
短期	急性	低级	人工	无限	非正式

3. 名形词、形动词　Nominal adjectives; adjectival verbs

名形词是兼有名词和形容词的语法特征的词。例如：

Nominal adjectives have the grammatical properties of both nouns and adjectives. For example:

精神　科学　困难　痛苦　秘密

方便　和平　矛盾　危险　理想

道德　团结　毒

形动词是兼有形容词和动词的语法特征的词。例如：

Adjectival verbs have the grammatical properties of both adjectives and verbs. For example:

明白　丰富　端正　习惯　讲究

肯定　平均　满意　集中　麻烦

冷淡　纯洁　可怜　深入　激动

讨厌　便宜　累　省　饿　活　死

四、名词、动词、形容词的主要区别 Important distinctions of nouns, verbs and adjectives:

	名　词	动　词	形容词
数量词＋	＋	－	－
副　词＋	－	＋	＋
不　＋	－	＋	＋
很　＋	－	－	＋
重　叠	AA 式	ABAB 式	AABB 式
带宾语	－	＋	－
作主谓宾语	常作主宾语	常作谓语	常作谓语

说明　Notes:

1. 名词主要能受数量词修饰，不能受"不"修饰。动词能带宾语，一般不能受“很”修饰。形容词能受副词修饰，不能带宾语。

Nouns may be qualified by numeral measure words but cannot be qualified by 不 . Verbs may take an object but cannot be qualified by 很 . Adjectives may be qualified by adverbs but cannot take an object.

2. 有些动词既能受“很”修饰又能带宾语。例如：

Some verbs, however, may be qualified by 很 and also take an object.

很念了几年书。

很有经验。

很解决问题。

但是，“很 + ～”不能单说，这些动词能带宾语，所以，不是形容词。

But 很 + ～ cannot be used alone; these verbs can take objects so they are not adjectives.

3. 能放入“很 + ～ + 宾语”格式里的是动词，如“喜欢”“想念”等。既能放入“很 + ～”格式里，又能放入“～ + 宾语”格式里，但是不能放入“很 + ～ + 宾语”格式里的词是兼类词。例如：

Those which can be used in the structure 很 + ～ + 宾语 are verbs, e.g. 喜欢，想念. Those which can be used in the structure 很 + ～ or ～ + 宾语, but not in the structure 很 + ～ + 宾语 are double classified words. For example:

很委曲　　委曲了你

很端正　　端正态度

很苦　　别苦了孩子

“委曲、端正、苦”等都是兼类词，受“很”修饰时是形容词，带宾语时是动词。

委曲，端正，苦 are all double classified words, which are adjectives when qualified by 很, and are verbs when taking objects.

练　　习

一、下列各词中，哪些是名词，哪些是动词，哪些是形容词：

月亮	足球	安全	客气
好看	健康	紧张	实际
理想	成功	担心	大量
丰收	放弃	改革	干净
感谢	关心	害怕	回信
幻想	寂寞	减少	交流
结束	经济	精神	介绍
考察	开除	厉害	漂亮
普通	前进	情况	缺少
设计	交际	条件	同意
完成	想像	结果	消息
新鲜	严重	增加	证明
观众	关系	自动	努力

二、下列形容词都能重叠吗？请写出它们的重叠形式：

安静	寂寞	宝贵	尖锐
悲观	简单	长久	精彩
诚实	辛苦	纯洁	老实
聪明	厉害	大方	马虎

发达	美好	方便	难看
腐败	平常	高兴	普通
合理	奇怪	欢乐	轻松
积极	软弱	及时	深刻
实在	舒服		

三、选词填空：

1. 我相信一个人的习惯是完全可以(　　)的。(改变、变化)

2. 生命在于(　　)。(活动、劳动、运动)

3. 他对那个售货员的服务态度很不(　　)。(满意、满足)

4. 上大学是我唯一的(　　)。(愿望、希望、渴望)

5. 再过几天,我就要和中国朋友(　　)了。(分别、分离、区别)

6. 你不要轻易(　　)他说的话。(信任、信赖、相信)

7. 他的生活很(　　),每天除了学习还是学习。(简单、单调、孤单)

8. 不要把哲学看得很(　　)。(秘密、严密、神秘)

9. 对那些破坏交通秩序的现象要(　　)。(禁止、阻止、制止)

10. 教育工作是(　　)的。(高贵、高等、高尚)

11. 他很有礼貌地(　　)了别人的邀请。(拒绝、谢绝、断绝)

12. (　　)理论研究是错误的。(忽视、轻视、歧视)

13. 打针以后,你有什么(　　)吗?(反映、反应)

14. 他的病已经(　　)了危险期。(脱离、摆脱)

15. (　　)森林是每个公民的责任。(保卫、保养、保护)

16. 我从来没有(　　)过这么热的天气。(经验、经历、经过)

17. 去年国庆节,北京(　　)了庆祝大会。(进行、实行、举行)

18. 他年龄大了,不(　　)做这种工作。(合适、适合、适当)
19. 战争夺去了他(　　)的生命。(贵重、珍贵、宝贵)
20. 全县人民的生活有了很大(　　)。(改进、改善、改良)

四、分辨形容词和区别词:

新式(　　)　　安全(　　)　　普通(　　)
中程(　　)　　微型(　　)　　复杂(　　)
平等(　　)　　长途(　　)　　超级(　　)
聪明(　　)　　紧张(　　)　　高速(　　)
定期(　　)　　单纯(　　)　　必要(　　)
特约(　　)　　国产(　　)　　长久(　　)
专用(　　)　　人造(　　)　　沉重(　　)
公共(　　)　　半旧(　　)　　古老(　　)
方便(　　)　　中华(　　)　　有色(　　)
光明(　　)　　特别(　　)　　不规则(　　)
非军事(　　)　　严重(　　)　　洁白(　　)
黄色(　　)　　无名(　　)　　细心(　　)

第六节　数词和量词
Numerals and Measure Words

一、数词　Numerals

意义:表示数目。例如:

Definition: Express numbers

〇　一　二　三　四　五　六　七　八

九 十 百 千 万 亿 半 两

零 壹 贰 叁 肆 伍 陆 柒 捌

玖 拾 佰 仟 万 亿

在汉语中,数词只表示抽象的数的概念,在计数时,数词后边须加上量词。

In Chinese, numerals express only the abstract concept of numbers. When counting, a measure word must be added to the numeral.

数词分基数词和序数词。

Numerals are divided into cardinal and ordinal numbers.

基数词 Cardinal numbers: 一、二、三、四、五、六 ……

(位数词 multiple digits: 个、十、百、千、万、亿)

序数词 Ordinal numbers: 第一、第二、第三、第四……

二、量词 Measure words

意义:表示事物的单位或动作的计量单位。例如:

Definition: Express units of objects or units of measurement of activity. For example:

个 种 座 条 件 棵

下 次 场 趟 回 遍

量词分名量词和动量词。

Measure words are divided into nominal and verbal types.

名量词表示事物的单位。例如:

Nominal measure words express units of objects. Examples:

个 支 张 件 条 把

动量词表示动作的量。例如:

Verbal measure words express units of measurement of activity. Examples:

次　下　回　遍　趟　场

名量词和动量词都有借用的。

There are borrowed measure words for both nominal and verbal types.

借用的名量词有：

The following are borrowed nominal measure words:

一手油　一缸水　一碟菜　一箱子书

一屋子烟　一车西瓜　一肚子话

借用的动量词有：

The following are borrowed verbal measure words:

看一眼　喝一口　踢一脚

（身体某一部分 parts of the body）

吃一碗　切一刀　打一枪

（工具 tools）

想一想　说一说　换一换

（重复动作 duplicated action）

数量词的特点　Characteristics of numeral measure words:

1. 可以直接修饰名词。

May modify nouns directly.

三十人　五十斤苹果　一架飞机

2. 可以代替名词。

May take the place of a noun.

喜欢吃就买二斤。

3. 可以作主语、宾语。

May serve as subjects or objects.

三十个(人)去西安。

昨天又来了十几个(留学生)。

4. 可以作谓语。

May serve as predicates.

他二十二岁。

你一本,我一本。

5. 重叠后可以作状语。

When repeated, may serve as adverbials.

他一口一口地吃着。

你把衣服一件一件叠好。

书要一本一本地看。

三、"二"和"两" 二 and 两

"二"和"两"都表示相同的数目,但用法不同。

二 and 两 express the same number, but their use is different.

二:

1. 可以单说。

Can be used alone.

2. 可以说"十二" "一百零二"。

One can say 十二,一百零二 .

3. 可以说"二十" "二百" "二千" "二万"。

One can say 二十, 二百, 二千 and 二万 .

4. 可以说"第二"。

One can say 第二 .

5. 后面一般不跟量词,不能说"二件" "二条"。

Usually may not be followed by a measure word. One can't say

二件,二条 .

两:

1. 不能单说。

Can't be used alone.

2. 不能说"十两" "一百零两"。

One can't say 十两,一百零两.

3. 不能说"两十",可以说"两百" "两千" "两万"。

One can't say 两十,but can say 两千,两万 .

4. 不能说"第两"。

One can't say 第两 .

5. 后面可跟量词,如"两件" "两条"。

May be followed by a measure word, e.g. 两件,两条 .

四、"多"和"少" 多 and 少

都表示数量。

Both express quantity.

1. 能作谓语 May serve as predicates:

人多 书少

能作状语 May serve as adverbials:

多看 少上街

能作补语 May serve as complements:

说得多 做得少

2. 受"很""不"的修饰。

May be qualified by 很 and 不 .

3. 可以指代名词。

May refer to nouns.

买了很多(书)

买了不少(水果)

五、概数 Approximate numbers

意义:表示大概的数目。例如:

Definition: Expressing approximate numbers. Examples:

两三(个)　七八十　十八九

二三十(岁)　五六十(年)

十来(个人)　三十来(岁)　一百来(里路)

十多(个)　三十多(岁)

三十五六(岁)〔*三十五多(岁)〕

第七节　时间词和方位词
Time and Position Words

一、时间词 Time words

意义:表示时间概念。例如:

Definition: Time words express the concept of time. Examples:

今天　昨天　明天　后天　去年　明年

现在　过去　从前　将来

当时　后来　以前　以后

但是表示时间概念的不一定都是时间词。例如:

Not all expressions which contain the concept of time are time words, however. For example:

立刻　马上　已经　赶快　　　　　　(副词 adverbs)

一会儿　三点　六小时

　　　　(数量结构 numeral measure word construction)

时间词不等于表示时间的名词。例如:

Time words are not the same as nouns which express time. For example:

春天　　夏季　　黄昏　　夜间

早上　　下午　　中午　　晚上

星期天　国庆节　中秋　　春节

这些词后边可以加“了”,能受时间词的修饰。例如:

These words may be followed by 了 and they may be modified by time words. For example:

星期天了。

今天早上。

去年秋天。

时间词能作主语、宾语,不受量词结构的修饰。例如:

Time words may serve as subjects, objects, and are not modified by measure words. For example:

今天星期三。

不要忘了过去。

*每个明天

*一个从前

二、方位词　Position words

意义:表示方向位置。包括单纯方位词和合成方位词。

Definition: Express direction and position. Position words include simple position words and compound position words.

单纯方位词有 Simple position words：

上　下　左　右　前　后　里　外

东　西　南　北　中　间　旁

合成方位词有附加和复合两类：

Compound position words include those with affixes and combinations.

附加　Affixes：

以上　以内　以前　以东

之上　之内　之前　之间

上边　里头　前面　左边

复合　Combinations：

上下　里外　东西　前后　中间

方位词不等于表示处所的名词。例如：

Position words are not the same as nouns which express place. Examples：

地方　饭厅　广场　上海

方位词不选择量词。例如：

Position words do not have designated measure words. Examples：

三本里头　五条里头　十把里头

方位词受量词结构的修饰，量词结构指代的是名词，而不是方位词。例如：

When position words are qualified by a measure word construction, the thing referred to is a noun, not the position word. For example：

三本里头（"三本"指代"书"　三本 refers to 书）

三本里头有两本是新的。

方位词的用法 The use of position words:

1. 单用(一般限于对应使用)。

Used alone (in comparisons only)

上有天堂,下有苏杭。

他左看看,右看看,还是想不起来。

前怕狼,后怕虎。

2. 可以放在名词前,也可以放在名词后。

May precede or follow nouns.

东门　里屋　上半天　前几年

门后　院外　三天内　年后

3. 有些方位词放在名词、动词后表示时间。

Some position words are used after nouns and verbs to express time.

一小时前　三天左右　他走后　上课中间

方位词"上下""左右""前后"用在时间名词或数量词之后,表示大概的时间或大概数量。

When the position words 上下,左右,前后 are used after time nouns or numerals, they express approximate time or quantity.

上下:三十上下　五米上下　二十公斤上下

左右:三十(岁)左右　五米左右　二十公斤左右

十点左右　五天左右

前后:"十·一"前后　春节前后　五点前后

方位词表 Chart of Position Words

单纯方位词	合成方位词					
	附加					复合
	以～	之～	～边	～面	～头	
上	以上	之上	上边	上面	上头	上下
下	以下	之下	下边	下面	下头	
前	以前	之前	前边	前面	前头	前后
后	以后	之后	后边	后面	后头	
东	以东		东边	东面	东头	东西
西	以西		西边	西面	西头	
南	以南		南边	南面	南头	南北
北	以北		北边	北面	北头	
里			里边	里面	里头	里外
外	以外	之外	外边	外面	外头	内外
内	以内	之内				
左			左边	左面		左右
右			右边	右面		
中		之中				中间
间		之间				
旁			旁边			

练　　习

一、在括号里填上适当的量词：

一(　　)山　　　　一(　　)河　　　　一(　　)面包

一(　　)星	一(　　)手	一(　　)纸
一(　　)刀	一(　　)衣服	一(　　)石头
一(　　)树	一(　　)路	一(　　)帽子
一(　　)眼镜	一(　　)葡萄	一(　　)牛
一(　　)井	一(　　)桥	一(　　)画儿
一(　　)笔	一(　　)汽车	一(　　)事
一(　　)计划	一(　　)飞机	一(　　)轮船
一(　　)诗	一(　　)文章	一(　　)绳子
一(　　)血	一(　　)伞	一(　　)裤子
一(　　)屋子	一(　　)花园	一(　　)火车
一(　　)马	一(　　)学校	一(　　)戒指

二、在括号内填上单纯方位词:

1. 室(　　)禁止吸烟。
2. 楼(　　)停着几辆出租汽车。
3. 路(　　)车辆很多,行人也很多。
4. 天空(　　)飘着个大气球。
5. 城(　　)比城(　　)热闹。
6. 两个月(　　)我还在国(　　)。
7. 他课(　　)的书也看,课(　　)的书也看。
8. 他眼(　　)只有自己,没有别人。
9. 课(　　)休息十分钟。
10. 路(　　)种满了树。

三、在括号内填上合成方位词:

1. 上午十点(　　),他到了机场。
2. 听课的有四十人(　　)。
3. 国庆节(　　),北京街上十分热闹。
4. 他已经是五十岁(　　)的人了,哪能和年轻人比呢!
5. 我如果十二点(　　)不来,你就不要等了。

6. 他每天看报纸,国(　　)的事情他都知道。

7. 他把屋子(　　)都收拾得整整齐齐的。

8. 昆明湖(　　)有个岛,叫龙王庙。

9. 猪八戒照镜子,(　　)不是人。

10. 限你十天(　　)造出箭来。

11. 长江(　　)是北方,长江(　　)是南方。

12. 北大(　　)有座塔。

13. 他(　　)为难,不知道去好还是不去好。

14. 同学(　　)要互相友爱,互相帮助。

15. 他家住在村(　　)。

16. 天气预报广播:三天(　　)有大雨。

17. 电影院门口的牌子上写着"一米(　　)的儿童谢绝入场"。

18. 他虽然点了点头,谁知道他心(　　)同意不同意呢!

19. 我的绘画水平在他(　　)。

20. 有的国家马路上的汽车靠(　　)行驶,有的国家马路上的汽车靠(　　)行驶。

第八节 代　　词

Pronouns

意义:指示或替代名词、动词、形容词、数量词或短语。代词的语法性质跟它所替代的词的语法性质一样。

Definition: Words which may indicate or take the place of

nouns, verbs, adjectives or numerals and measure words are called pronouns. The grammatical properties of a pronoun are the same as the word it represents.

分类 Categories:

1. 人称代词 Personal pronouns

我 你 他 我们 你们 他们 咱们

大家 别人 自己 您

"咱们"包括听话人在内,常用于口语。"我们"有时不包括听话人。有时"我们"指说话本人自己,如文章中用"我们认为……",实际只指代写文章的人自己。

咱们 includes the listener, mostly used in spoken language; 我们 does not include the listener. Sometimes 我们 refers to the speaker himself or herself. For example, if an essay says 我们认为, it is actually referring to the writer.

指人的名词可以加"们"(如:人们、朋友们)。指人的名词不加"们"时,不一定表示单数(如:同学来了)。

Nouns which refer to people may take the suffix 们 (as 人们, 朋友们), but nouns not using 们 are not necessarily singular (as 同学来了).

"人家"可以指说话本人自己,也可以指第三者。例如:

人家 may refer to the speaker or to a third person. For example:

你怎么才来?人家都等了你半天了。

(指说话者 refers to the speaker)

不是我不同意,人家不同意我也没办法。

(指别人 refers to others)

2. 指示代词 Demonstrative pronouns

这(近指 near)　那(远指 far)

每、各(个体)(individual)

某(不定)(indefinite)

这儿　那儿　这里　那里	(指代地点 refer to place)
这会儿　那会儿	(指代时间 refer to time)
这么　那么 这样　那样 这么样　那么样	(指代行为、性状、程度 refer to behavior, state, or degree)

"这""那"可以直接修饰名词。例如:

这 and 那 may directly qualify nouns. For example:

这梨多少钱一斤?

那箱子里装的是什么?

"这、那、每、各、某"都能跟量词组成量词结构。例如:

这,那,每,各,某 may all be used with measure words as part of a measure word construction. For example:

这个　那次　每件　各条　某种

"这么、那么、这样、那样"修饰动词时,表示动作的方式。例如:

When 这么,那么,这样 and 那样 qualify verbs, they denote the manner of the action. For example:

这么画才对呢!

就这样办吧!

"这么、那么、这样、那样"修饰形容词时,表示程度。例如:

When these same words qualify an adjective, they express degree. For example:

几年不见,你都长这么高了。

他是那样的大方、热情。

“这样、那样、这么样、那么样”做谓语时，表示行为或动作。例如：

When used as predicates，这样，那样，这么样，那么样 express behavior or action. For example:

别这样！

不让他那样他偏那样。

就这么样吧。

3. 疑问代词　Interrogative pronouns

谁　什么　哪　哪儿　哪里　几

多少　多会儿　怎么　怎样　怎么样

“谁”指代人。“什么”指代事物。“哪”后边可以跟量词(如：哪个)。“哪儿、哪里”指地点。“几、多少”指数量。“多会儿”指时间。“怎么、怎样、怎么样”指事物的性状、程度或动作的方式，可以作谓语。它们既可以表示任指，也可以表示虚指。

谁 refers to people，什么 to things. 哪 may be followed by a measure word (哪个). 哪儿，哪里 refer to place. 几，多少 refer to quantity. 多会儿 refers to time. 怎么，怎样，怎么样 refer to state, degree or manner of action and may be used as predicates. Their indication can be general or indefinite.

任指(表示周遍意义)　General (including everything):

谁也别走。

我什么也不想吃。

这儿比哪儿都好。

给多少我也不要。

我怎么说他也不听。

虚指(无所指或指不出来)　Indefinite (non-specific):

咱们上街去买点什么。

谁想去谁去。

哪儿也不想去，就愿呆在家里。

挤什么挤？

金钱算什么？

我们说代词的语法性质跟它所替代的词的语法性质一样，只能是基本上一样。实际上存在着不一致的情况。“什么”是指代名词的，语法性质应该和名词相一致，可是，“什么”还可以指代动词或形容词。例如：

We say that the grammatical characteristics of pronouns is the same as that of the words they represent. They are the same basically, but in fact there are some differences. 什么 represents a noun so the grammatical characteristics should be the same as nouns; however, 什么 can also represent verbs and adjectives. Examples:

你看什么？——我看跳舞。

你怕什么？——我怕冷。

4. 每、各

共同点 Similarities of 每 and 各：

(1) 都指组成全体的任何一个个体。

Both refer to any of the individual.

他对每个人都很热情。

他每天都跑步。

每年学校开一次运动会。

(2) 都能和量词合用。

Both can be used with measure words.

每个　每班　每位

各个　各班　各位

不同点　Differences:

(1)"每"强调个体之间的共性,"各"侧重个体之间的不同。试比较下列句子:

每 emphasizes the general characters of the individual units. 各 emphasizes the differences in the individual units. Compare the following examples:

每个人都去长城了。
每次看电影他都不来。
每个地方他都去过。

各人有各人的事。
各国的情况不一样。
各个民族的服装都不同。

(2)"每"不能直接修饰名词("每月、每人、每星期、每小时"除外),"各"能直接修饰名词。

每 cannot directly qualify nouns while 各 can. Exceptions are 每月,每人,每星期,每小时.

每(一)件事　每句话　每本书　每个季节

各国　各民族　各工厂　各单位　各学校

但是"各"直接修饰名词受限制,常和下列量词结合:

But 各 has certain restrictions when directly qualifying nouns; it is commonly used with the following measure words:

各种　各位　各条　各类

各门　各项　各级　各界

(3)"每"还可以修饰动词。每 can also directly qualify verbs.

每到春天,花都开了。

每逢节日的时候，她总是打扮得漂漂亮亮的。

5. 某

(1) 指代确定的人或事。还可以指代时间、地点。

Represents a definite person or thing; can also represent time or place.

某人　某事　某天　某地

他说的某人我也知道。

去年，我们去江西某地参观。

有时，"某"直接放在姓氏之后指确定的人。

Sometimes 某 is placed immediately after a surname to refer to a given person.

王某　　李某　　张某

王某人　　李某人

张某某　　（王××）

(2) 可以重叠。

Can be repeated.

某某人　某某公司　某某出版社

(3) "某"后加量词修饰名词。

A measure word can be placed after 某 to qualify a noun.

某种原因　某项工程　某个人

由于某种原因，我不能去旅行了。

这样做不符合学校的某项规定。

(4) "某"也指不确定的人或事物。

某 can also refer to an indefinite person or thing.

某人曾提出过这项建议。

某个城市曾发生过这类怪事。

我们要做好准备，以免发生某种情况。

练　习

一、填上适当的疑问代词：

1. 请问，去动物园(　　)走？
2. 这是(　　)天的报纸？
3. (　　)公园好玩就去(　　)公园。
4. 他的病现在(　　)了？
5. 你到北大(　　)年了？
6. 公共汽车站在(　　)？
7. 一辆轻便自行车(　　)钱？
8. 电影(　　)时候开演？
9. (　　)想去(　　)去。
10. 你这是(　　)啦？

二、用疑问代词改写下列各句：

1. 他不饿，一点东西也不想吃。(什么)
2. 我找了很久，就是找不到外文书店。(怎么)
3. 人人都说他是个好人。(谁)
4. 你要的那本书到处都能买得到。(哪儿)
5. 刚到北京来的时候，觉得样样都很新鲜。(什么)

三、指出下列各句中的疑问代词表示的是任指还是虚指：

1. 谁听了都会高兴的。
2. 这有什么值得吹的。
3. 你从哪儿来？
4. 你喜欢买什么就买什么。
5. 我想买点什么礼物送给朋友，可是又不知道买什么好。

6. 我也不知道他在跟谁说呢!

7. 你最好哪儿也别去。

8. 给多少钱他也不卖。

9. 我难道什么也没说吗?

10. 他怎么也不相信我说的话。

四、选词填空:

(一) 每　各　某

1. 老师让我们(　　)人讲一个笑话。

2. 他们约定在(　　)个地点见面。

3. (　　)种情况都可能发生,你要做好准备。

(二) 我们　咱们

4. 不必客气,(　　)都是自己人。

5. (　　)除了上课以外,还经常出去参观。

6. 在(　　)之间,没有什么不能解决的问题。

第九节　副词、介词、连词

Adverbs, Prepositions and Conjunctions

一、副词　Adverbs

意义: 表示动作或状态的程度、范围、时间、否定、重复等。

Definition: Express degree, range, time, negation or repetition of behavior or state, etc.

分类　Categories:

程度副词 Adverbs of degree：很、太、挺、更、最、极、顶、十分、非常、再$_1$、特别、格外、尤其、极其、相当 、稍微

范围副词 Adverbs of range：都$_1$、也、全、单、光、仅仅、一共、净、独、就、统统

时间副词 Adverbs of time：刚、就、还$_1$、先、正、立刻、马上、总是、忽然、已经、一时

否定副词 Negatives：不、没有、未、别、莫

重复副词 Adverbs showing repetition：又、再$_2$、还$_2$、再三、常常、经常、往往、反复

语气副词 Adverbs of mood or tone：偏偏、简直、索性、未免、究竟、明明、的确、反正、却、倒、也许、居然、几乎、好在、果然、到底、难道、何尝、都$_2$

功能 Function：

1. 修饰动词和形容词。

Qualify verbs and adjectives

刚走。　　刚好。

已经来了。　　已经晚了。

非常想家。　　非常高兴。

形容词也能修饰动词。可是，形容词能单说，能修饰名词，能作谓语；副词不能单说，不能修饰名词，不能作谓语。例如：

Adjectives may also qualify verbs. While adjectives can be used alone, can qualify nouns, and can be predicates, adverbs cannot be used alone, cannot qualify nouns, and cannot be predicates. Examples:

真走还是假走？　　（副词 adverb）

好天气。　快！　他穷。　（形容词 adjective）

有些副词是借用的形容词，两者意义完全不同。试比较：

Some adverbs are derived from adjectives, but the meaning is completely different. For example:

白帽子　白去(相当于"空"　equivalent to 空)
光脚　光说空话(相当于"只"　equivalent to 只)
老朋友　老抽烟(相当于"总是"　equivalent to 总是)
好天气　好冷(相当于"十分"　equivalent to 十分)
怪脾气　怪难看的(相当于"挺"　equivalent to 挺)
硬卧车　硬要去(相当于"非……不可"　equivalent to 非…不可)
直路　直笑(相当于"不断"　equivalent to 不断)
特别快车　特别有意思(相当于"非常"　equivalent to 非常)

类似的还有"经常""干脆""偶然""确实"等。

Other examples are 经常,干脆,偶然,确实,etc.

2. 少数副词能修饰名词、代词和数量词。

A few adverbs may qualify nouns, pronouns, and numeral measure words:

就你一个人会。
光他知道。
就这么办。
他刚二十岁。
今天才星期五。
他走了没几天。

少数副词兼有两类以上副词的语法性质。例如:

A few adverbs have the grammatical characteristics of more

than one adverb category. For example:

再
- 程度(degree): 再好也没有了。
- 重复(repetition): 过一会儿你再来。

都
- 范围(range): 都谁去?
- 语气(tone): 都十二点了。

才
- 程度(degree): 才学了一点儿。
- 范围(range): 他来了才两个月。
- 语气(tone): 他才不愿意呢。

有些名词、动词、形容词加上"地"以后,具有副词的功能。

Some nouns, verbs, and adjectives function as adverbs when they are used with 地.

(1) 历史地　本能地　善意地　策略地

(2) 公开地　批判地　习惯地　统一地

(3) 高兴地　仔细地　经常地　严肃地

单音节形容词重叠后加"地",功能同于副词。例如:

When monosyllabic adjectives are repeated and followed by 地, they function as adverbs. For example:

好好地　快快地　远远地　深深地

有的副词能加"地"。例如:

Some adverbs can be followed by 地. For example

非常地　十分地　忽然地　简直地

渐渐地　统统地　格外地　稍稍地

除个别副词(未必、也许、不、大概)外,不能单说。

With only a few exceptions, adverbs cannot be used alone.

少数副词能修饰副词。例如:

A few adverbs can qualify other adverbs. For example:

不一定　也常常

少数副词可以作补语。例如：

A few adverbs can be complements. For example:

冷得很　考虑再三

二、介词 Prepositions

介词的作用在于同名词、代词或名词性词组组成介词结构作状语，修饰动词。

The function of a preposition is to form prepositional structure with a noun, a pronoun, or a noun phrase to qualify a verb.

1. 从动词演变而来。大部分仍保留着动词的功能。例如：

Most prepositions which came from verbs still retain their verbal functions. For example:

在　到　给　跟　比　替

动词	他在家。	介词	在墙上画画。
	到北京了。		到上海开会。
	给我一支烟。		给我打一针。
	他总跟着我。		你跟谁说话？
	咱们比一比。		我比你高。

2. 介词表示的意义

Sense or meaning expressed by prepositions:

在北京上大学。　(处所 place)

从明天开始。　(时间 time)

用笔写字。　(方式 method)

为人民服务。　(目的 goal)

比我打得好。　(比较 comparison)

跟我说话。　　　　（关系 relation）

把门关上。　　　　（处置 managing）

被大家发现了　　　（被动 passive）

3. 分类（根据作用）　Categories (based on function):

引出施事者　Introduce the actor：被、让、叫

杯子被他打破了。

鱼让猫吃了。

车子叫小王骑走了。

引出受事者　Introduce the object being acted：把

我把衣服洗了。

你把他当外人。

小王把车骑走了。

引出与事　Introduce the one being related：跟、给、对、为、比

我跟他借钱。

你给我翻译。

你对他说吧。

别为我担心。

他比我年轻。

引出工具　Introduce the tool：用、以

用机器生产。

以他为榜样。

引出处所、时间　Introduce the place, time：在、到、从、于

在旅馆住	在六月上演
到商店买东西	到上个月结束
从上海来	从今年开始
于北京病逝	于上个月回国

有的介词结构可以作定语。例如：

Some prepositional constructions can be attributives. For example:

对儿童的教育是十分重要的。

关于灾情的报告已经写好了。

三、连词 Conjunctions

意义：能够连接词、词组、分句或句子的词叫连词。

Definition: Words which can join words, phrases, clauses, or sentences are called conjunctions.

分三类 There are three types:

第一类：连接词或词组。

Those which connect words or phrases are:

和 跟 同 及 与 或(者)

第二类：连接分句或句子。

Those which connect clauses and sentences are:

A: 不但 不管 不论 无论 即使
尽管 哪怕 虽然 因为 只有
只要 要是 假如 与其 宁可

B: 不过 从而 否则 何况 可见
所以 因此 因而 然而 但是

第三类：既能连接词、词组，又能连接分句。

Those which can connect words and phrases as well as clauses are:

并 并且 或者 而且 还是
除非 以及 而 既 又

第一、三类中大部分表示联合关系，第二类的大部分表示主从关系。

这种划分主要根据两条：一是连词，二是语意轻重。

Most of those in groups one and three are coordinators, while most in group two are subordinators. This type of division is primarily based on two criteria: 1, the conjunction; 2, semantic tone.

1. 第一类连词　Conjunctions of the first type

跟印欧语里连词(如俄语中的"v"，英语里的 and，法语中的 et)相比，"和"在用法上有很大限制。

Compared to Indo-European conjunctions ("u" in Russian, "and" in English, "et" in French) 和 is very restricted in usage.

(1) "和"只能连接词和词组，不能连接句子。

It can connect only words and phrases but cannot connect sentences. Examples:

男职工和女职工一样。

坐车去和骑车去都行。

长江和黄河是我国最大的两条河。

他和我都是北京人。

(2) "和"在连接词和词组时也受到限制。

When connecting words and phrases, it is restricted.

他更加勤奋和努力地工作。

应该提高阅读和写作的能力。

产品的数量和质量都有了很大提高。

会议讨论和通过了"九·五"计划。

大力宣传和提倡计划生育。

事情正在进一步地调查和了解。

"和、跟、同、与"既是连词，又是介词。

和,跟,同 and 与 are conjunctions and prepositions as well.

连词{
他和老王见过面了。
我跟老王商量过了。
你同老王一块去。
语言教学与研究。

介词{
他和你没个完。
我跟他开玩笑。
你同他说没有用。
与困难作斗争。

区别连词"跟"和介词"跟":

Distinguish conjunction 跟 from preposition 跟:

甲跟乙+{
对称性动词:握手、交换、结婚、比赛、见面、商量
非对称性动词:借钱、开玩笑、发脾气、讲理

(1) 连词"跟"前后成分可以颠倒,意思不变。

Components preceding and following the conjunction 跟 may be reversed without affecting the meaning.

(2) 介词"跟"前可以插入别的成分,如"昨天""一定"等。

Other components may be inserted before the preposition 跟, e.g. 昨天,一定,etc.

(3) 连词"跟"前后组成联合结构,介词"跟"带宾语与动词组成偏正结构。

The components before and after the conjunction 跟 form a coordinative construction. The preposition 跟 takes an object and forms an endocentric construction with the verb.

连词"或(者)"表示一种选择关系。

The conjunction 或(者)expresses a relationship of choice.

你们什么时间来都可以,或者明天,或者后天。

人固有一死,或重于泰山,或轻于鸿毛。

2. 第二类连词 Conjunctions of the second type

都是连接复句中的分句的。

复句中的分句与分句之间在意义上是有联系的,这种联系在形式上主要是通过连词来体现的。连词是作为一种语法手段而不是作为结构成分出现的。

The conjunctions of the second type connect clauses of complex sentences. The clauses in a complex sentence are connected in terms of their meaning. This type of relationship is expressed through conjunctions. Conjunctions are used as a kind of grammatical method but not as a constructual element.

因为他病了,所以没来上课。

虽然人很多,可是并不热闹。

不但他会唱,而且大家都会唱。

有的连词只能出现在头一个分句里,而有的连词只能出现在第二个分句里。

Some conjunctions can appear only in the first clause; other conjunctions can appear only in the second clause.

A类:连词在头一个分句里。

Type A: Conjunctions in the first clause:

不管天气多冷,他也要去。

无论你说什么,他都不听。

既然你答应了人家,你就应该做。

B类:连词在第二个分句里。

Type B: Conjunctions in the second clause:

天气不太好,所以我没去。

东西是便宜,不过送人不太合适。

你要按时来，否则我们不等你。

C类：连词既可以出现在第一个分句中，也可以出现在第二个分句中。

Type C: Conjunctions which may appear in the first as well as the second clause:

{我们就这么办，要是你不反对的话。
要是你不反对的话，我们就这么办。

{他还是买了一台彩电，尽管他经济上不太富裕。
尽管他经济上不太富裕，他还是买了一台彩电

{所以出现这次事故，是因为我们思想麻痹。
因为我们思想麻痹，所以出现了这次事故。

有的连词还可以出现在主谓语之间。

Some conjunctions may even appear between subject and predicate.

{如果你有时间，请到我家来玩。
你如果有时间，请到我家来玩。

{虽然他去了，可是什么也没看见。
他虽然去了，可是什么也没看见。

{不但我不信，连大家也不信。(大家不信)
我不但不信，连想也没想过。(我不信)

3. 第三类连词 Conjunctions of the third type

举"而"为例：

For the third group 而 will be used as an example:

(1) 表示并列 Showing coordination:

朴素而大方 简短而有力

(2) 表示转折 Showing transition:

少而精　华而不实

(3) 表示方式　Expressing form:

江水滚滚而来　大风呼啸而过

(4) 表示承接　Expressing continuation:

战而胜之　取而代之

其他连词举例如下　Here are some more conjunctions:

他在会上发了言,并且在报上发表了文章。

他去过那个地方,并不认为那儿的天气热。

你什么时候走都可以,或者这个星期,或者下个星期。

来参观的人非常多,工人、大学生以及小学生都来了。

她既不是演员,又不是服装模特,但穿着总是很讲究。

练　习

一、在下列各句的括号内填上适当的副词:

1. 你先走,我(　　) 就去。
2. 他都二十几了,可是(　　)像个孩子。
3. 不让你去,你(　　)要去。
4. 秋后,天气(　　)冷了。
5. 我(　　)以前在哪儿见过他。
6. 这么大的事,你(　　)不知道?
7. 从那次分别后,我们(　　)也没见过面。

8. 我给他去过几封信，可是他(　　)没给我回过信。

9. 他去年就出国了，你(　　)知道。

10. 你要是再不来，你(　　)永远也别来。

二、在下列各句的括号内填上适当的介词：

1. 人类社会的发展是(　　)低级到高级。

2. 中国有句成语叫做(　　)猫画虎。

3. (　　)旅行计划，我们下一次再商量。

4. 你是(　　)哪个国家来的？

5. 昨天，他的自行车(　　)撞坏了。

6. (　　)上课，我们还要完成作业。

7. 你(　　)电话号码告诉我，有事我给你打电话。

8. (　　)治好他的病，我几乎跑遍了所有的医院。

9. 我们要(　　)一切有经验的国家学习。

10. 我(　　)流行音乐没有兴趣。

三、在下列各句的括号内填上适当的连词：

1. 他(　　)有房子，还有汽车。

2. (　　)他以前学过中文，(　　)很少有机会说。

3. (　　)你有时间，欢迎你到我家来做客。

4. (　　)你同意了，就应该说话算数。

5. 我(　　)他以前不认识。

6. (　　)你下功夫学，就一定能学好。

7. 北京夏天(　　)很热，(　　)时间不长。

8. 我(　　)明天走，(　　)后天走。

9. (　　)你现在坐飞机去，也来不及了。

10. (　　)那里的条件再苦，他也愿意去。

第十节 助 词
Auxiliaries

助词是一个特殊词类。它附着在词、词组上，表示某种附加意义。

Auxiliary is a special word class. It adheres to other words or phrases showing some additional meanings.

助词按功能分为三类：

They are divided into three groups according to function:

1. 结构助词　Structural auxiliaries：的、地、得、所、等、似的
2. 动态助词　Aspect auxiliaries：了、着、过
3. 语气助词　Tonal auxiliaries：啊、吧、呢、吗、了、的、么

一、结构助词"的、地、得" The structural auxiliary 的(地，得)

1. "的"

(1) "的"字结构修饰名词。

The 的 construction qualifies nouns.

你的票
我的哥哥
木头的桌子　} 名(代)+中
姑娘的心事
圆的面积

走的人
看的书
昨天来的信
下车的地点
买来的水果 } 动＋中

新的生活
漂亮的衣服
火热的心
蓝蓝的天
老老实实的人 } 形＋中

对顾客的态度
关于你的作品 } 介宾＋中

你走的时间
他住的地方
大家提的意见 } 主谓＋中

(2)"的"字结构还可以限制、指代名词。

The 的 construction can restrict or take the place of a noun.

我的行李重，你的轻。
我的自行车坏了，借你的骑一下。 } 能代替(can replace the noun)

我的工作很轻松。
我的意见你都知道。 } 不能代替(cannot replace it)

新的(衣服)很贵。
聪明的(人)不那样做。 } 能代替(can replace it)

冷的感觉。
简单的回答。 } 不能代替(cannot replace it)

说话的(人)
他翻译的(文章)　} 能代替(can replace it)

喝茶的时候
他翻译的技术　} 不能代替(cannot replace it)

不能代替的原因是这类偏正结构的中心语都是表示抽象概念的名词。

The reason why it cannot substitute is that the head words in this type of endocentric construction are nouns which express abstract ideas.

2. "地"

"地"字与动词、形容词、副词、名词、数量词、代词及其他词语组成"地"字结构,修饰动词或形容词。

地 can form 地 construction with a noun, a numeral, a pronoun, a verb, an adjective, an adverbial or other words and phrases to qualify verbs or adjectives.

动＋地:感动地说、(雨)不停地下、批判地吸收

形＋地:谦虚地笑了、愉快地接受、随便地问、认真地讨论

很＋形＋地:很远地来了、很轻松地放下、很快地完成

形重叠＋地:好好地干、高高兴兴地走了、冷冷地看了一眼

副＋地:渐渐地冷了、特别地生气、故意地开玩笑

名＋地:科学地分析问题、历史地看一个人

数量＋地:一个一个地解决

代＋地:这样地处理了

3. "得"

动词、形容词加上"得",后面跟补语,指出动作的结果或程度。

When a verb or an adjective takes 得 followed by a complement, it shows the result or degree of the action.

看得远　　做得完　　走得出去

好得很　　高兴得跳起来

说得大家都笑了

4."的"字结构的功能　The function of the 的 construction

(1) 作主语、宾语、定语　As subject, object, attributive:

你说的有道理。

你的笔坏了,用我的吧!

今天的报在哪儿?

(2) 作谓语　As predicate:

这帽子我的。　　行李谁的?

这苹果酸的。　　地上湿的。

头发乱七八糟的。　　心里怪难受的。

电影票他买的。　　这话谁说的。

(3) 作补语　As complement:

长得胖胖的　　擦得亮亮的

跑得满头大汗的　　累得上气不接下气的

二、动态助词　Aspect auxiliaries

1."了"

动词词尾(后缀),表示完成。它可以出现在各种不同时间的句中。

A verb suffix expressing completion. It may occur in sentences of any tense.

今天我写了一封信。
他从市场买来了几条鱼。
写完了我才去看朋友。
(现在时 present tense)

春节我们放了三天假。 (过去时 past tense)

放了假我们就可以去旅行了。

(将来时 future tense)

我买了票就走。 (未然 future completed)

我买了票就走了。 (已然 completed)

我走了十分钟就到了。

(完成后发生 occurrence after completion)

你走了十分钟他就来了。

(未完成就发生 occurrence before completion)

2."着"

(1) 动词词尾(后缀),表示动作或状态的持续。

A verb suffix expressing continuation of action or state.

谈着话　唱着歌　写着字

(动作的持续 continuation of an action)

门开着　表走着　水流着

(状态的持续 continuation of a state)

留着小胡子　光着脚　秃着头

(非动作动词+着,状态的持续 continuation of a state)

(2)"动词+着+动词",可以表示动作的方式或手段与目的的关系。

Expressing the relationship between the ways or means of actions and purposes.

微笑着说　含着泪走了　卷着大葱吃

(方式 way)

急着赶火车　忙着收拾东西

(第二个动作表示目的 the second action

shows purpose)

还可表示第一个动作正在进行中出现第二个动作。

It also expresses the second action occurs during the progression of the first action.

说着就哭了起来

哭着哭着睡着了

走着走着摔了一跤

(3) "形容词+着",表示程度高。

An adjective +着 expresses a high level or degree.

菜热着呢　　生活好着呢

天冷着呢　　屋子小着呢

注意:"着"表示动作的进行,和时间没有关系。例如:

Note: 着 expresses the progression of an action and is not related to time.

昨天我正看着电视,一位朋友来了。

(过去 past)

外边刮着大风。　　(现在 present)

明天我们散着步再谈。　　(将来 future)

如果商店还开着门,你帮我买盒烟。

(假设 conditional)

3. "过"

动词词尾(后缀),表示曾经有过的经历。

A verb suffix expressing a past experience.

我去过西安。

我找过他两次。

他学过中文,没学过英文。

他吃过苦。

他有过光荣的历史。

吃过午饭,我们就出去了。

也可用于将来经历的动作或假定要经历的动作。

Can also be used in action of future experience or suppositional experience.

明天你吃过早饭来找我。

(将来经历 future experience)

要是你没有看过这个电影,应该看看。

(假设经历 suppositional experience)

4.“了”和“过”的区别 Differences between 了 and 过

(1) 语法意义不同。

The grammatical meaning is not the same.

我们去了长城。 (完成 completed)

我们去过长城。 (经历 experienced)

(2) 结果不同。

The result is not the same.

他当了演员。 (现在是演员 still is an actor)

他当过演员。 (现在不是演员 not an actor now)

我学了英语。 (学会了 learned)

我学过英语。 (不一定会 may not know it now)

(3) 否定形式不同。

The Negative form is not the same.

我没去西安。 (“了”去掉 了 is left out)

我没去过西安。 (保留“过” 过 remains)

三、语气助词 Tonal auxiliaries

表示语气。用于句末,轻读。

Express mood or tone. Used at the end of a phrase, spoken lightly.

1. “了”

(1) 表示情况发生了变化。有成句和表达语气的作用。

Expresses change in situation or condition. It has the function of completing a sentence or showing a tone.

下雨了。	(发生了 happened)
快上课了。	(将要发生 will happen)
信我看过了。	(完成 completed)
大家不说了。	(停止 pause)
老张病了。	(状态变化 change of state)
他不想去了。	(意愿变化 change of will)
休息了。	(开始 start)
我走了。	(将要发生 will happen)
我已经买了机票了。	(既表完成又表变化 completion and change)
秋天了。	(名词+了 noun+了)
这双鞋小了。	(形容词+了 adjective+了)
不好了。	

(2) 表示肯定。

Shows certainty.

他走了。

我会开汽车了。

2. “的”

(1) 表示肯定,加强语气。

Shows certainty with a stronger tone.

他会来的。

他以前学过的。

我写的。

我花钱买的。

我问过他的。

(2) 表示已然。

Expresses completion.

我骑车去的。

他昨天到的。

你什么时候毕业的?

注意:一种语气可以有几个语气词来表示,一个语气词可以表示几种不同的语气。

Note: A mood or tone can be expressed by different tonal auxiliaries. and a tonal auxiliary can express different mood or tones.

3."啊(呀、哇、哪)"

"啊""呀""哇""哪"是同一个语气词,只是写法不同。这是由于受前一个音节的影响。

These are actually one and the same auxiliary in different written forms, which are decided by the previous syllable.

(1) 啊:

单说: 啊! 大海。

－ng 后:原来是老张啊!

－i[1]后:多好的孩子啊!

－i[ʅ]后:多好的同志啊!

(2) 呀: －ɑ、－e、－i、－o、－uo、－u、－ü 后

谁拿来的花呀?

这是谁的车呀?

你呀,就知道说大话。

你不信佛呀？

你说的是我呀？

你进屋呀。

好大的鱼呀！

(3) 哇：－u、－ou、－ao后

快出哇！

走哇！

真高哇！

谁家的猫哇？

(4) 哪：－n后

你要小心哪！

天哪！

“啊(呀、哇、哪)”的主要作用　Main functions of 啊(呀，哇，哪)：

(1) 表示疑问。　Showing interrogation.

人哪？

这里没羊啊？

什么时候走哇？

谁会骑马呀？

(2) 表示提醒。　Showing reminding.

考试时，别紧张啊。

走哇，时间不早了。

(3) 表示劝告。　Showing advice.

你可当心哪！

4.“呢”

(1) 表示疑问。　Showing interrogation.

这是怎么回事呢？

你的书包呢？

他怎么不来呢？

你呢？

(2) 表示反问。 Asking back.

我没来过北京，怎么知道它的样子呢？

他帮了我很大的忙，怎能不感谢他呢？

(3) 表示商量。 Showing discussion.

你是去上海呢还是去西安呢？

坐车去还是骑车去呢？

(4) 表示对比。 Showing contrast.

我才不像他呢！

颐和园去过，香山还没去过呢。

(5) 表示假设。 Showing preposition.

他要是不来呢？

天要是下雨呢？

我不同意呢？

5. "吧"

(1) 表示祈使。 Expressing imperative.

你就去吧！

这件事你就答应了吧！

走吧！别等了。

(2) 表示劝告。 Expressing advice.

你说吧！

还是别听他的吧！

这么好的东西，买了吧！

(3) 表示同意。 Expressing agreement.

就这么办吧!

好吧!

(4) 表示揣测。 Expressing guess.

这件事你不会不知道吧!

今天可能会下雨吧!

你是日本人吧!

我去你不会反对吧!

6. "吗"

(1) 表示疑问。 Expressing interrogation.

你去过香山吗?

你会说中国话吗?

你是第一次来中国吗?

(2) 表示反问。 Asking back.

你不是去过故宫了吗? }(分辩)
我说过这种话吗?

这么简单的道理你就不懂吗? }(责怪)
你这样做像话吗?

练 习

一、在下列句子的括号内填上适当的语气词:

1. 出租汽车来了(　　)?
2. 这么大的事情,你不会不知道(　　)?
3. 你这样对待你的朋友,太不像话(　　)。

4. 我以为是谁(　　)? 原来是你(　　)。

5. 你只要把道理讲给他,我想他会听(　　)。

6. 你家的小花猫(　　)?

7. 去(　　),大家都在等你(　　)。

8. 万一他回不来(　　)?

二、指出下列各句中语气助词表示什么语气:

1. 他在哪儿呢? (　　)

2. 买呢,太贵;不买呢,太可惜。(　　)

3. 这件事你就放心吧。(　　)

4. 我不是告诉过你了吗? (　　)

5. 电话打给他了,他不会不来的。

6. 你快点把照片拿出来让我们看看吧。

7. 你怎么不早说呢?

8. 哭又有什么用呢?

三、在括号里填上适当的"了""着""过":

1. 这孩子小时候没吃(　　)奶。

2. 你等(　　)瞧吧,将来有好戏看。

3. 去年他一次都没到我家来(　　)。

4. 铁人王进喜在工地上吃(　　)吃(　　)睡着了。

5. 人到(　　)这个世界上总想做点什么。

6. 说(　　)他拿(　　)一块蛋糕吃(　　)起来。

7. 我走(　　)不少地方,就是没到(　　)西藏。

8. 他怕我走不动,还扶(　　)我走(　　)一段路。

9. 我是今年才到中国的,春节我还没过(　　)。

10. 长征途中,连马皮都成(　　)难得的美味了。

四、改正下列句子中的错误:

1. 昨天晚上,你们看不看电影?

2. 昨天晚上,我们没看了电影?

3. 他每天都上课了。

4. 你有多少中文书吗？

5. 去年他来了中国，今年他又来着中国。

第十一节　词的兼类
Double Classification of Words

汉语里有少数词既具有这类词的语法功能，又具有那类词的语法功能。这样的词叫兼类词。例如：

In Chinese some words have the grammatical functions of more than one class. These words are called words of double classification. For example:

科学 { 名词——自然科学
形容词——很科学

破烂 { 名词——卖破烂
形容词——破烂东西

端正 { 动词——端正态度
形容词——态度端正

下面列举的都是兼类词：

The following are words of double classification:

计划	陪同	证明	组织	命令	说明
展览	报告	代表	认识	胜利	限制
要求	改善	保证	爱护	发明	麻烦
教育	纪念	开始	习惯	区别	休息

信任　运动　决定　批评　工作　病

词的兼类现象跟分析词义有联系。例如：

The phenomenon of double classification is related to analysis of word meaning, for example:

死{死了人(失去生命)——动词
死脑筋(不灵活)——形容词

从词义上看是一个词，从语法上看是两个词。因此，兼类词是指意义相关，但是具有不同词类语法功能的词。

如果一个词所包含的两个意义不同，彼此又无联系，我们只能把它们看成同音词。例如：

From the standpoint of meaning it is one word; from the standpoint of grammar it is two words. So words of double classification are words with related meaning, but different functions. If a word has two different meanings which are not related, we classify them as homonyms. For Example:

会{开会
会唱歌　　白{白纸
白吃

花{一朵花
花钱　　信{信件
信不信

第十二节　词的构成

Composition of Words

语法分为词法和句法两部分。词法研究的是词的内部构造，以语素为基本单位。句法研究的是句子的内部构造，以词为基本单位。

Grammar is divided into morphology and syntax. Morphology is the study of the internal composition of words with the morpheme as the basic unit. Syntax is the study of the internal composition of phrases with the word as the basic unit.

一、单纯词和合成词 Simple words and compound words

（一）单纯词是由一个语素构成的。单纯词多数是单音节的，但也有双音节的，多音节的。

Simple words are composed of one morpheme. Most simple words have only one syllable, but there are some with two syllables or multiples syllables.

人　马　喝　我　好

葡萄　玻璃　玫瑰　胡同　马虎

巧克力　尼古丁　法西斯

奥林匹克　阿司匹林　歇斯底里

（二）合成词是由两个或两个以上的语素构成的。

Compound words are composed of two or more morphemes.

人民　马匹　唱歌　我们　好看　花儿

构词法主要指的是合成词的构造方式。汉语构词方式主要有三种：重叠式、附加式、复合式。

Morphology refers primarily to the composition of compound words. There are mainly three ways: repetition, affixing, compounding.

1. 重叠式 Repetition

名　词：爸爸　妈妈　哥哥　姐姐　弟弟　妹妹
爷爷　奶奶　姥姥
星星　宝宝　娃娃
人人　年年　天天　月月

量　词：个个　张张　本本　件件(作主语)

动　词：想想　看看　写写(AA)
打听打听　休息休息　活动活动(ABAB)

形容词：好好儿的　小小儿的　红红儿的(AA儿的)
大大方方　干干净净　漂漂亮亮　老老实实　客客气气　整整齐齐(AABB)
古里古怪　糊里糊涂　啰里啰嗦　马里马虎
土里土气　慌里慌张(A里AB)
通红通红　雪白雪白　冰凉冰凉(ABAB)
红通通　亮晶晶　冷冰冰　暖洋洋(ABB)

副　词：常常　刚刚　明明　偏偏　白白　渐渐　稍稍

2. 附加式　Affixing

前加：初　老　第　小

初：初一　初二　初三　……　初十
老：老虎　老鼠　老鹰　老王　老张　老李
第：第一　第二　第三
小：小姐　小鬼　小菜儿

后加：子　儿　头　们　者　性　家　化

子：桌子　刀子　刷子　胖子　包子
儿：花儿　款儿　画儿　瓶儿　铃儿
头：木头　石头　舌头　前头　吃头　苦头

们：我们　你们　朋友们　作家们
（* 几位老师们　* 很多人们）
者：文节工作者　爱国主义者
性：现实性　代表性　可能性　长期性
艺术性　特殊性　感性　弹性
家：画家　作家　科学家　发明家　歌唱家
书法家　军事家
化：现代化　商业化　工业化　美化　软化
净化

3. 复合式　Compounding

并列式：人民　朋友　国家　道路　根本　道德
斗争　生产　来往　开关　休息　买卖
是非　奇怪　伟大　光明　上下　迟早
东西　刚才　而且
偏正式：飞机　月饼　白菜　大衣　火车　电话
小看　重视　冰凉　好看　难听
动宾式：满意　出版　卫生　怀疑　有限　关心
动员　主席　告别　带头　讨厌　负责
无效　得罪　因此
动补式：证明　扩大　改良　感动　减少　说明
提高　降低　更正
主谓式：心疼　面熟　例如　春分　年轻　眼红
饼干　火烧　水利　油漆
其　他：

名＋量：
- 纸张　船只　车辆　信件　布匹
- 人口　房间　书本　线条　花朵

简称 ——北大　政协　人大　联大　外长
　　　——三废　四化　五讲四美　六书

二、词和非词的界限　Boundaries of words and non-words:

1. 词　Words: 饭碗、雨伞、马路、电视、火车、粗心、小看、手表、钢笔、花生米

2. 词组　Phrases: 木头房子、我哥哥、山东省、白纸、红铅笔、理发、洗干净、快走

3. 既可能是词,又可能是词组　Those which could be words or phrases: 火烧、买卖、东西、狐狸尾巴

1、2 两类容易分,3 类要具体分析。只根据意义不能划分清楚,要从结构上去分析。复合词不能扩展,如"白菜"不等于"白的菜","铁路"不等于"铁的路"。如果组成成分都是自由语素,可能是词(如:白菜、铁路、小米、牛肉、鸡蛋、大楼),可能是词组,也可能既是词又是词组(如:火烧、买卖、东西)。词的意义不是组成成分的意义的相加,如"大方"不等于"大"加"方"、"海味"不等于"海"加"味"。

Groups 1 and 2 are easy to differentiate. Group 3 requires detailed analysis. The differentiation cannot be based only on meaning. There must be an analysis of the structure. Compound words cannot be extended. For example, 白菜 is not the same as 白的菜, 铁路 is not the same as 铁的路. If the components are all free morphemes, it could be a word or a phrase, or a word as well as a phrase. The meaning of a word does not equal to the adding of the meanings of the components. For example, 大方 doesn't equal to 大 plus 方, 海味 doesn't equal to 海 plus 味.

练　　习

一、指出下列各词的构造方式：

篮球(　　)	教育(　　)	控制(　　)
金鱼(　　)	开放(　　)	事件(　　)
居民(　　)	华侨(　　)	合同(　　)
合作(　　)	海洋(　　)	改善(　　)
发展(　　)	多余(　　)	办理(　　)
访问(　　)	体育(　　)	放弃(　　)
民主(　　)	光明(　　)	选择(　　)
照片(　　)	问题(　　)	市场(　　)
村子(　　)	妻子(　　)	线条(　　)
酒杯(　　)	花朵(　　)	房间(　　)
人大(　　)	政协(　　)	鸽子(　　)
老鼠(　　)	娃娃(　　)	刚刚(　　)

二、指出下列合成词的构造方式：

庆祝	国家	刚才
坚持	年轻	无期
买卖	改善	白菜
光明	缩小	精神
例如	合理	友谊
飞机	希望	外语
运动	怀疑	雪白
交换	月饼	姓名

三、举例说明什么是同音词，什么是兼类词。

第二章　句法结构
Chapter 2　Syntactic Structure

第一节　什么是句法结构
What Is Syntactic Structure?

我们说的每句话都是由词按一定的句法规则组成的。不同的句法规则造成了不同的句法结构。

Everything we say is made up of words which are put together according to specific rules of syntax. Different rules of syntax creates different syntactic structure

一句话长的有几十个词,是不可能一下子从词到句子的。词和词之间有一种组合关系,按一定的结构关系组成比词大的东西,我们把它叫作句法结构。

It is improbable that a portion of speech consisting of some twenty or more words simply forms itself into a sentence. There is a kind of relationship of combination which exists among words. Because of these specific syntactic relationships, words can be combined into a larger unit. We call this syntactic structure.

这种句法结构单说时是句子,处在句子中是词组。换句话说,就是词组和句子都是句法结构存在的具体形式。可见，词组的句法结构关系和句子的句法结构关系是完全一样的。这是汉语语法里的一个重要特点。

When such a structure is independent, it is a sentence; when it is part of a sentence, it is a phrase. In other words, phrase and sentence are both concrete forms of syntactic structure. The relationships of syntactical structure are the same for sentence and for phrase. This is an important characteristic of Chinese grammar.

第二节　句法结构的基本类型
Basic Types of Syntactic Structure

根据句法结构内部组成成分之间的关系，我们可以把它分为五种类型。

Based on the relationships of the elements within a phrase, we can identify five types of structure.

聪明人	修饰关系 modifying
	偏正结构 endocentric structure
看电视	支配关系 dominating
	述宾结构 verb object structure
说清楚	补充关系 complementing
	述补结构 verb complement structure
他同意	陈述关系 commenting
	主谓结构 subject predicate structure

面包牛奶　　并列关系 coordinating

联合结构 the compound structure

这五种结构类型是汉语句法结构的基本形式,下面我们分别介绍这五种句法结构。

These five structural types are the basic forms of Chinese syntax. Below we will introduce the five types separately.

一、偏正结构 The endocentric structure

偏正结构的前一部分叫修饰语,后一部分叫中心语。前一部分修饰或限制后一部分。

The first part of the endocentric structure is called the qualifier, the second part is known as the head. The first part qualifies or limits the second part.

第一组:聪明人　　酸苹果　　(性质 quality)

玻璃杯　　塑料袋　　(质料 material)

我的信　　他哥哥　　(领属 possession)

三块钱　　五匹马　　(数量 quantity)

第二组:很喜欢　　仔细地研究

(程度、方式 degree, way)

在门口等　　从右边走

(处所、方位 place, location)

马上去　　已经晚了　　(时间 time)

不好　　没看见　　(否定 negation)

从上面两组例子中可以看出:

From the above two groups of examples it is clear that

1. 修饰语表示各种意义。

Qualifier can express all kinds of meaning.

2. 有的修饰语和中心语之间可以加"的"。

的 can be used between some qualifiers and their heads.

3. 回答问题"什么的～""谁的～""多少～""怎么样地～"。

It is used to answer such questions as 什么的～,谁的～,多少～,and 怎么样地～.

所不同的是第一组里的中心语是名词,第二组里的中心语是动词或形容词。这是因为语法功能不同。第一组不能用"不"来否定,第二组可以。第一组里的修饰语在句子中称作定语,第二组里的修饰语在句子中称作状语

The difference is that in the first group the head word is a noun, in the second group the head word is a verb or an adjective. This is due to the difference in grammatical function. The first group cannot be negated with 不,the second group can. The qualifiers in the first group are called attributives in a sentence. The qualifiers in the second group are adverbials in a sentence.

二、述宾结构 The verb object structure

述宾结构的前一部分叫述语,后一部分叫宾语。述语表示动作或行为,宾语表示跟动作相关的事物,两者之间是一种支配、影响的关系。

The first part of this structure is the verb; the second part is the object. The verb expresses action or behavior. The second part expresses whatever it is that is associated with the verb. The relationship between the two is one of governing or effect.

修车　　洗衣服　　(受事 patient)

看戏　　听广播　　(对象 object)

坐火车　　乘飞机　　（工具 tool）

买东西　　盖房子　　（结果 result）

晒太阳　　淋雨　　（施事 agent）

去上海　　出国　　（处所 place）

述宾结构中的述语可以跟“了”“着”，不改变结构关系。

有的述宾结构中间可以插入“的”，变成偏正结构。例如：

The verb in the verb object structure may be followed by 了 or 着 without changing the structure. If a 的 is added in the middle of the verb object structure, it becomes an endocentric structure. For example:

写的信　　买的东西　　看的电视

述宾结构的类型很多，有些并不表示动作或行为，而是表示某种状态变化。例如：

There are many types of verb object structure. Some do not actually express action or behavior, but show a kind of change in condition. For example:

有人　像谁　下雨　姓王

三、述补结构 The verb complement structure

“洗衣服”是述宾结构，宾语“衣服”是“洗”的对象。“洗干净”是述补结构，补语“干净”是“洗”的结果。

洗衣服 is a verb object structure, in which 衣服 is the object of 洗. 洗干净 is a verb complement structure, in which 干净 is the complement and the result of 洗.

同一个动作可以得到不同的结果。例如：

The same action may have different results. For example:

洗完了　洗旧了　洗白了　洗坏了　洗丢了

同样的结果也可以由不同的动作来完成。例如：

The same result could also be obtained from two different actions. For example:

洗干净　刷干净　擦干净　扫干净　弄干净

前一部分叫述语，后一部分叫补语。补语补充或说明前面的述语。

The first part is the verb; the second is the complement. The complement completes or clarifies the verb.

补语往往补充说明动作产生的结果、程度、可能和趋向。例如：

The complement usually completes or clarifies the result, degree, probability, and the direction of an action.

洗干净　说清楚　写完　(结果 result)

洗得很干净　急得哭了　好得很　(程度 degree)

洗得干净　说不清楚　写得完　(可能 probability)

走出来　跑过来　唱起来　(趋向 direction)

四、主谓结构　The subject predicate structure

主谓结构由主语和谓语两部分组成。主语是说话人陈述的对象，谓语是对主语的陈述，说明主语怎么样或是什么。

The subject predicate structure is composed of two parts: the subject and the predicate. The subject is what the speaker is talking about. The predicate is the comment on the subject, explaining how or what the subject is.

(1) 你去　我知道　他愿意　(施事 agent)

(2) 天气好　事情多　年龄大　（性状 character）

(3) 书丢了　电影演完了　问题解决了

（受事 patient）

(4) 今天星期五　他是校长　你三本

（无所谓施受 neither agent nor patient）

(1)(3)例中主语和动词之间是一种施受关系，(2)(4)不是。

The examples in (1) and (3) have a kind of actor-receiver relationship. Those in (2) and (4) do not.

特征　Characteristics:

1. 主语在前，谓语在后。

Subject is followed by predicate.

2. 主语可以是体词或谓词，谓语一般只能是谓词性成分。

The subject may be a nominative or predicative, but the predicate normally can only be a predicative type.

3. 主语和谓语之间有停顿。

There is a pause between subject and predicate.

4. 主语和谓语之间可以插关联词，如"要是、如果、虽然、即使"等。

A connector can be inserted between subject and predicate, e.g. 要是，如果，虽然，即使，cet.

5. 谓语可以变成反复问句(正反问句的形式)。

The predicate can become a repeated question (a rhetorical question).

五、联合结构　The compound structure

几个成分并列，地位平等，不分主次，这种结构叫联合结构。

When several elements which are parallel appear together, it is a compound structure. For example:

太阳和月亮　飞机、轮船和火车　北京、天津、上海　春、夏、秋、冬　(名词)

干净整齐　聪明大方　短平快　多、快、好、省　(形容词)

学习讨论　研究解决　传帮带　听说读写　(动词)

组成联合结构的各部分意义不同,先后次序有差别。组成部分不限于两个,可以是三个、四个。

从组成成分看,可以分为两种:并列和选择。

The different parts of a compound structure have different meanings and there is a difference in order. The parts are not limited to two, but may be three or four. There are two types of combination: coordinative and alternative.

并列　coordinative:

你和他　来去

选择　alternative:

你或者他　来不来

第三节　复杂的句法结构
The Complex Syntactic Structure

包含两种以上结构关系的句法结构一般称为复杂句法结构。

五种句法结构可以重复或交替形成复杂结构。例如：

Syntactic structures which include two or more structure relationships are usually called complex syntactic structures. The five types of syntactic structure can be used repeatedly or in turn. For example:

历史的经验和教训
看过小说和电影
搬进来一户人家
大胆地进行经济改革
唱起歌跳起舞
买了一件上衣一条裤子
你去他去都一样

下面列表归纳这五种基本句法结构：

The following is a chart of the five basic syntactic structures:

结构类型	语义关系	组成成分	主体位置	可插入成分
偏正结构	修饰	两部分	主体在后	插入“的”
述宾结构	支配	两部分	主体在前	插入“了”“着”
述补结构	补充	两部分	主体在前	插入“得”
主谓结构	陈述	两部分	平等	插入“是不是”
联合结构	并列 选择	等于 大于 } 2	平等	插入“和”“或” “并”“还是”

第四节　层次分析法

Component Analysis

从上面的情况中，我们发现从词到词组到句子，完全是由这五种基本句法结构一层一层组织起来的，复杂的句子不过是这五种结构的交替和重复。

From the above illustrations we can see that from word to phrase to sentence, all are built by using these five basic syntactic structures. Complex sentences are simply formed by using these structures repeatedly or alternately.

句子内部构造是有层次性的。我们分析句子就要按它内部的构造逐层分析，了解其结构层次和结构关系。例如：

Sentence structure has several levels. In analyzing sentence we must analyze the structure level by level and understand the relationship of these levels. For example:

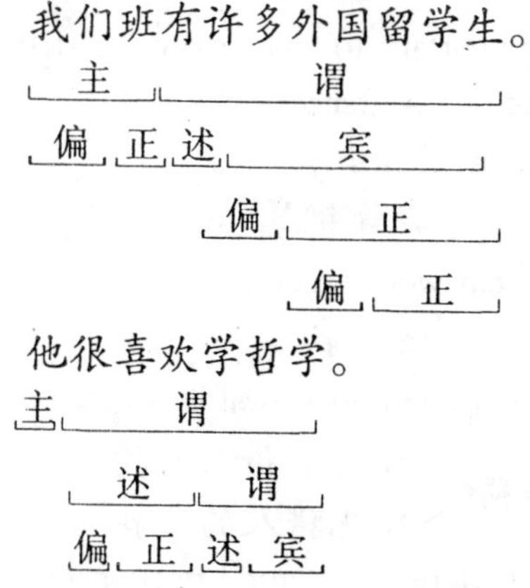

这种根据句子内部的层次构造来逐层分析句子的方法叫层次分析法。

This method of analyzing sentence structure according to its level is called component analysis.

同一个语言片段可以分出不同的结构层次：

The same portion of speech can be divided into different structural levels.

两个大学的研究生　　我讲不好

偏　正　　主　谓

偏　正　　主　谓

层次构造相同，结构关系不一定相同：

Though the structural level may be the same, the structural relationships may not be the same.

一朵大红花　　小张上公园

偏　正　　主　谓

偏　正　　述　宾

可见弄清句子的结构关系和意义是十分重要的。

It is therefore very important to make clear the structural relationships and the meaning of a sentence:

1．成分不同　Different element:

他弹钢琴　　我弹钢琴

2．词序不同　Different word orders:

我问他　　他问我

3．层次结构不同　Different structural levels:

咬死猎人的狗 < 咬死 ‖ 猎人的狗 / 咬死猎人的 ‖ 狗

4．结构关系不同　Different structural relationships:

学习文件 ＜ 述宾结构 / 偏正结构

5. 重音和停顿不同　Different pauses and stresses:

一年就生产五万斤 ＜ 重音在"一年"指生产多 / 重音在"就"指生产少

练　　习

一、仿例指出下列句法结构的类型：

学习语法(述宾)	条件很好(主谓)
发展经济(　　)	天气预报(　　)
体育运动(　　)	国际比赛(　　)
接受意见(　　)	山东济南(　　)
新闻广播(　　)	工业生产(　　)
历史研究(　　)	出租汽车(　　)
西安洛阳(　　)	经济改革(　　)
经济困难(　　)	控制人口(　　)
积极参加(　　)	我画不好(　　)
学习努力(　　)	服务项目(　　)
学习时间(　　)	打听清楚(　　)

二、仿例指出下列偏正结构里的修饰语是定语还是状语：

新衣服(定语)	仔细看(状语)
非常事件(　　)	慢镜头(　　)
刚才的情况(　　)	非常舒服(　　)
两块饼干(　　)	两次进城(　　)
突然的消息(　　)	突然地死去(　　)

白白地浪费(　　)	白白的墙(　　)
慢走(　　)	真好(　　)
刚开始(　　)	怪脾气(　　)
大胆的计划(　　)	大胆地想(　　)
高高的个子(　　)	高高地举起(　　)
叮叮当当的声音(　　)	叮叮当当地响(　　)

三、按下列结构分别举两个例子：

1. 主谓结构
2. 述宾结构
3. 修饰语是状语的偏正结构
4. 带“得”的述补结构
5. 不带“得”的述补结构
6. 表示选择关系的联合结构

四、用层次分析法分析下列句子：

1. 天气渐渐冷了。
2. 我最喜欢的是书。
3. 我很喜欢看电影。
4. 今天我请客。
5. 他说得大家笑了。
6. 他对人很热情。
7. 去不去都一样。
8. 今天比昨天冷。
9. 他人小心不小。
10. 去年没有下过雪。

第三章　句　　子
Chapter Three　Sentences

第一节　什么是句子
What Is a Sentence?

我们说话是一句一句说的,写文章也是一句一句写的。可见,句子是说话的单位,是交流思想的基本表达单位。

一句话,不论长短,只要单独成立,同时能表达一定的意思就是一个句子。

When we speak, we speak phrase by phrase, sentence by sentence. It is the same with writing. So sentences are units of speech, and basic units of expression for communicating. A phrase, no matter long or short, if it can stand independently and express a definite idea, is a sentence.

每个句子有一定的语调,表达一个相对完整的意思,句子与句子之间有较大的停顿。书面上一般用句号、问号、叹号隔开。

Each sentence has a specific intonation and expresses a complete idea. Between sentences, there is a distinct pause (a comma or a full stop is used in writing).

句子的主要特征在于它的表述性,词和词组不具备这一特征。这是词、词组和句子的区别。

The important feature of a sentence is its predicative nature. Words and phrases do not have this feature. This is the difference between words, phrases and sentences.

构成句子的条件有三个:

There are three conditions for forming a sentence:

1. 前后有停顿。

There must be a pause before and after.

2. 带有一定的语调。

Have a definite intonation.

3. 表示完整的意义。

Express a complete meaning.

一般人认为句子具有主语和谓语两部分。这是从逻辑上给句子下定义。其实句子并不限于判断句。在口语中,存在着大量的无主句(如:下雨了。)和省略句(如:我的眼镜呢?)。

Most people believe that a sentence must have a subject and a predicate. This is a logical definition of a sentence. But in fact sentences are not limited to such types. In spoken language there are many elliptical phrases (我的眼镜呢) and sentences without subjects (下雨了).

句子是由词或词组组成的,短的可以是一个词(如:"好。""我。")。这样,我们不能根据长短来决定是词还是句子。语素不一定比词短,词不一定比句子短,它们不是一个平面上的东西。作为句子必须具备上面所说的三个条件。

Sentences are formed with words or phrases. Short sentences may be only one word (好,我),and we can not determine whether it is a word or a sentence by its length. Morpheme are not necessarily shorter than words and words are not necessarily shorter than sentences. They are not items of the same class. Sentences must be defined by the three features listed above.

第二节　句子的类型
Sentence Types

按结构划分,句子可以分为主谓句和非主谓句两大类。

主谓句是由主谓结构形成的句子。非主谓句是由主谓结构以外的结构形成的句子。例如:

Based on structure, sentences can be divided into two types: subject-predicate sentences and non-subject-predicate sentences. Subject-predicate sentences are sentences formed with subject-predicate constructions. Non-subject-predicate sentences are formed with structures other than subject-predicate constructions. For example:

主谓句 Subject-predicate sentence	非主谓句 Non-subject-predicate sentences
你好。	好。
我去上海。	是我。
今晚有音乐会。	飞机。
铁是金属。	下雨了。
天女散花。	禁止吸烟。

下面的句子都不是非主谓句,而是省略句:

The following sentences are not non-subject-predicate sentences but elliptical sentences:

没有人不知道。　(省略主语 omit subject)

有点不舒服。　(省略主语 omit subject)

比我大三岁。　(省略主语 omit subject)

马上就来。　(省略主语 omit subject)

我的眼镜呢?　(省略谓语 omit predicate)

小王呢?　(省略谓语 omit predicate)

省略句中的省略成分能够补出来,而非主谓句是补不出来的。换句话说,省略句离开上下文不能独立成句,而非主谓句离开上下文能独立成句。

For the elliptical sentence it is possible to fill in the omitted element, but in a non-subject-predicate sentence it is not possible to do the filling in. In other words, an elliptical sentence cannot stand independently without the context, but a non-subject-predicate sentence can stand on its own without the context.

主谓句和非主谓句都是单句,两个以上单句形式可以组成复句。复句包括联合复句和主从复句。

- 句子
  - 单句
    - 主谓句
    - 非主谓句
  - 复句
    - 联合复句
    - 主从复句

Subject-predicate sentence and non-subject-predicate sentence are both simple sentences. Two or more simple sentences can make complicated sentences, which include compound sentence and endocentric sentence.

按照功能划分,句子可分为陈述句、祈使句、疑问句和感叹句四种。

Based on function, sentences can be divided into four types: declarative, imperative, interrogative and interjective.

1. 陈述句:说明一种事实。

Declarative sentence explains something.

我走了。

你穿得太少了。

他不在家。

今天星期五。

2. 祈使句:表达一种意志(请求、商量、命令、劝阻、警告等)。

Imperative sentence expresses volition (request, consultation, command, advice, or warning).

请坐。

明天和我一块去吧!

不许动!

你要小心哪!

3. 疑问句:表示某种疑问。又可分为三类:

Interrogative sentences express doubt. They can be further divided into three types:

(1) 特指问句(对句中某一部分提问) Reference questions (referring to a specific part in the sentence):

他是谁?

你看什么?

书店在哪儿?

今天星期几?

(2) 是非问句 Yes or no questions:

你去吗?

他买了吗?

你近来好吗?

(3) 选择问句　Alternative questions:

你是学生不是?

你去还是不去?

你喜欢不喜欢打网球?

三种问句的区别如下:

The differences among these three types are illustrated below:

	特指问句	是非问句	选择问句
用疑问代词	+	−	−
带"吗"	−	+	−
回答具体	+	−	+

4. 感叹句:抒发某种感情。

Interjective sentences express some kind of emotion.

火!　(惊讶 surprise)

活该!　(愤怒 anger)

爸爸回来啦!　(喜悦 joy)

车开得真慢呀!　(抱怨 complaint)

练　习

一、指出下列各句中哪些是主谓句,哪些是非主谓句:

时间就是生命。　(　　)

谢绝参观。　(　　)

有这样一个故事。　　(　　　)

面向未来。　　(　　　)

请进。　　(　　　)

没问题。　　(　　　)

二、指出下列各句，哪些是陈述句，哪些是祈使句，哪些是疑问句，哪些是感叹句：

墙上挂着几幅山水画。　　(　　　)

他今天很高兴。　　(　　　)

头发上也能刻诗吗？　　(　　　)

你就听他说下去吧！　　(　　　)

现在走来得及吗？　　(　　　)

秋天的香山真美！　　(　　　)

三、指出下列问句中，哪些是特指问句，哪些是是非问句，哪些是选择问句：

你什么时候走？　　(　　　)

你有亲人吗？　　(　　　)

你怎么不早告诉我？　　(　　　)

你见过大海吗？　　(　　　)

我的信吗？　　(　　　)

那座桥有多长？　　(　　　)

他姓李还是姓季？　　(　　　)

第三节　主语和谓语
Subjects and Predicates

一、主语和谓语

一个句子通常有两部分组成,或者说可以划分为两部分,即主语和谓语。主语是谓语陈述的对象,是话题;谓语是陈述主语的,两者之间是陈述关系。

A sentence is usually made up of two parts, or it can be divided into two parts: the subject and the predicate. The subject is what the predicate is about, is the topic. The predicate is what is posited about the subject. The relationship of the two is a declarative one.

下面我们对两种内容相同、结构关系不同的格式进行比较。

Below we will compare two patterns which have the same content, but different structural relations.

A	蓝蓝的天 穿西装的那个人	B	天蓝蓝的 那个人穿西装

"天"和"那个人"在A、B两组里都是被说明的对象。在A组,说明成分在前面,是一种修饰性的说明,整个结构是个偏正结构式的词组。在B组,说明成分在后面,是一种展示性的说明,整个结构是个主谓结构式的句子。我们把B组里的"天"和"那个人"都看作是话题,是主语,把后面的成分看作是对主语的陈述,是谓语。

In both A and B 天 and 那个人 are the things being talked

about. In A the descriptive part comes at the beginning of the phrase; it is a qualifying declaration. The whole structure is an endocentric phrase. In B the descriptive part comes at the end. It reveals something. The whole structur is a subject predicate type of sentence. We say that in group B 天 and 那个人 are thc topics, the subjects. The latter part is what is posited about the subject; it is the predicate.

主语既然是一种话题、陈述的对象，其范围可以很宽，可以指人、物，某种现象，某个事件，某种性质、属性，某种动作、行为等。

Since the subject is a kind of topic which the declaration is about, its range is very broad. It can refer to people, things, certain phenomena, affairs, qualities, ownership, action or behavior.

主语可以由名词、代词、数量词、形容词、动词等充任。例如：

The subject slot may be filled by nouns, pronouns, numeral measure words, adjectives or verbs. For example:

精神很好。　健康很重要。　（名词 nouns）

今天有会。　过去哪有这种事。

（时间词 time words）

北京到了。　上海见。　（处所词 location words）

你去哪儿？　他多大了？　（代词 pronouns）

三斤够了。　十米长了点。

（数量词 numeral measure words）

干净当然好。　大方有什么不好？

（形容词 adjectives）

胖胖的是小王。　甜丝丝的像蜂蜜。

（状态词 statives）

男二十，女十八。　彩色比黑白好。

（区别词，限于对比时出现 only used in comparison）

说又有什么用？ 去好还是不去好？

(动词 verbs)

你来又能怎么样？ 你去我不同意。

(主谓词组 subject-predicate phrase)

他买的是书。 我写的是诗。

("的"字结构 的 construction)

外面下雨呢。 前怕狼，后怕虎。

(方位词 location words)

谓语可以由动词、形容词等谓词性成分担任。名词、时间词、处所词、数量词、状态词等也可以作谓语。例如：

The predicate slot may be filled by such predicative elements as verbs or adjectives. Nouns, time words, location words, numeral measure words, or statives may also be predicates. For example:

我知道。 他答应了。 (动词 verbs)

价钱便宜。 您真糊涂。 (形容词 adjectives)

老王黄头发。 他日本人。 (名词 nouns)

今天星期二。 现在三点钟。

(时间词 time words)

下一站王府井。 航行终点重庆。

(处所词 location words)

每人两本。 他四十岁。

(数量词 numeral measure words)

自行车他骑走了。 他心眼好。

(主谓结构 subject-predicate structure)

眼睛大大的。 包子挺热的。 (状态词 statives)

树又高又大。 她漂亮大方。

(并列结构 coordinating structure)

在具体句子里,主语和谓语的关系是多种多样的。当谓语为动词性成分时,作主语的成分,从意义上说,可以是动作的发出者,即施事者;也可以是动作的接受者,即受事者。还有一种既不是施事者,又不是受事者。例如:

In actual sentences, there are many kinds of relationship between subject and predicate. If the predicate is a verb, then in terms of meaning, the subject is doing the acting as the agent. It could also be the recipient of the action, the patient. There is also a type in which the subject is neither agent nor patient.

Examples:

1. 施事主语句　The subject is the agent:

鸟飞了。

太阳出来了。

我走了。

他会画画儿。

2. 受事主语句　The subject is the patient:

票卖完了。

车修好了。

问题解决了。

杯子打破了。

3. 主语既不是施事者,又不是受事者　The subject is neither the agent nor the patient:

这是小麦。

我有事。

他在家。

这支笔不好用。

4. 主语既可能是施事者,又可能是受事者(限于指人的)

The subject may be the agent or the patient (referring to people only):

他不认识。
- 他不认识(别人)。 (“他”是施事　他 is agent)
- 不认识他。 (“他”是受事　他 is patient)

小王找到了。
- 是小王找到的。 (“小王”是施事者　小王 is agent)
- 小王被找到了。 (“小王”是受事者　小王 is patient)

他要动手术。
- 他要给别人动手术。 (“他”是施事者　他 is agent)
- 别人给他做手术。 (“他”是受事者　他 is patient)

二、两种特殊主语句　Two types of special subject sentence

除了施事主语句外,下面另外介绍两种主语句。

There are two other types of subject sentences.

(一) 受事主语句　Sentences with patient as subject.

主语是后边动作的受事。在意义上,主语是被动者,受谓语中行为动作的支配和影响。

The subject is the recipient of the action which follows. In meaning, the subject is being acted upon. It is affected and governed by the behavior or action expressed in the predicate.

A. 信写完了。
　 花浇过了。

B. 书我看完了。

信我寄走了。

C. 这瓶酒喝不了五个人。

这车能坐二十几个人。

特点 Characteristics：

1．表示被动意义（有的可加介词：被、让、叫）。

Shows a passive meaning (some can be followed by the preposition 被，让 or 叫).

他被人送进了医院。

车让人偷走了。

坏人给抓起来了。

2．主语是有定的或是有周遍性的。

The subject is definite or of a general nature.

东西找着了。
客人送走了。 } （有定 definite）

谁我也不认识。
什么我也不想看。 } （周遍 general）

3．谓语是复杂的，不是一个单个的动词。

The predicate is complex; it is not a simple verb.

东西拿走了。

衣服洗干净。

一件皮大衣可以穿十几年。

（二）主谓谓语句 Sentences with subject-predicate predicates

谓语是个主谓结构，这是汉语语法的一个特点。例如：

The predicate is a subject-predicate structure. This is a unique feature of Chinese. For example：

他心眼好。 英语是 His heart is good.

或是 He has a good heart.

英语里没有相应的结构形式。上句结构主语是 his heart,下句结构主语是 He。汉语里的“他心眼好”,也有人主张分析为“他的心眼好”。实际上,这是从意义上分析的。

English does not have a similar structure. The structural subject in the first sentence is “his heart”, in the second sentence“he”. Some scholars advocate analyzing the Chinese: 他心眼好 as 他的心眼好. In fact, this is a semantic analysis.

我们还可以从别的方面来考察。例如:

We can consider this from other angles, for example:

他精神真好。

主语“他”后可以停顿,而且可以插入其他成分(如:最近、从前),插入的其他成分只能属谓语部分。

One can pause after the subject 他. Furthermore, other elements can be introduced (最近,从前). Once other elements are added it can only be the predicate:

类型 Similar examples:

1. 小主语隶属大主语,小谓语一般是形容词。

The second subject is governed by the main subject; the predicate within the predicate is usually an adjective.

他力气可大了。

他胆小。

那孩子眼睛大大的。

2. 大小主语之间存在着施受关系,小谓语由动词充当。

There is an agent/patient relationship between the main subject and the second subject. The predicate within the predicate is a verb.

他中文说得很流利。

语法我以前没学过。

他什么都知道。

3. 大主语是时间词或处所词。

The main subject can be a time word or a locative.

今天商店不开门。

上海我没去过。

南方夏天雨多。

4. 小主语是数量结构,小谓语也由数量结构充当。

When the second subject is a numeral measure word, the predicate within the predicate is also a numeral measure word.

苹果一斤八毛。

他们两人一屋。

我们每人半斤。

5. 小主语指代大主语,小主语由代词充当。

When the second subject refers back to the main subject, the second subject is a pronoun.

实现四个现代化,这是中国人民的心愿。

你说的那个人,他在哪儿?

练 习

一、按下列要求举例(每种举两个):

1. 时间词作主语

2. 方位词作主语

3. 数量词作主语

4. 动词结构作主语

5. 形容词作主语

6. 主谓结构作主语

7. 述宾结构作主语

8. 述补结构作主语

9. “的”字结构作主语

二、指出下列各句的语义关系(施事、受事关系):

1. 他爱他的小儿子。

2. 信写完了没有?

3. 雨不停地下着。

4. 这是油画吗?

5. 我还没见过像他这样的人。

6. 工作条件改善了。

7. 桌上放着一个花瓶。

8. 花盆放在阳台上。

三、按下列要求举例(每种举两个):

1. 名词作谓语

2. 数量词作谓语

3. 状态词作谓语

4. 主谓结构作谓语

5. 联合结构作谓语

四、指出下列句子哪些是施事主语句,哪些是受事主语句,哪些是主谓谓语句:

1. 他唱京剧。

2. 信寄走了。

3. 这是小李的照片。

4. 酒不好喝。

5. 他胆大。

6. 表修好了。

7. 客人走了。

8. 他什么都吃。

9. 我身体不舒服。

10. 他妻子是医生。

11. 他去南京了。

12. 南京夏天很热。

13. 时间到了。

14. 他年龄大了,记性也坏了。

15. 他去上课。

16. 表停了。

第四节　述语和宾语
Verbs and Objects

一、述语和宾语　Verbs and objects

主语是对谓语说的,宾语是对述语说的。主语和宾语没有直接的联系。主语一定在谓语前头,宾语一定在述语后头。

A subject relates to a predicate. An object relates to its verb. Subjects and objects have no direct relationship to each other. A subject must come before the predicate. An object must follow the verb.

按句子的结构层次，主语和宾语不在一个平面上。主语和谓语在一个层次里，述语和宾语在一个层次里。例如：

According to levels of structure, subject and object do not belong to the same syntactic level. Subject and predicate belong to the same level; the verb and its object belong to the same level.

我 吃 桔 子

主 谓

述 宾

述语指的是谓语中的动词，表示动作或行为。宾语是动作或行为涉及的人和事物。述语和宾语之间在意义上的联系是多种多样的。

述语 refers to the verb in the predicate. It expresses action or behavior. The object is the person or thing affected by this action or behavior. Verbs and objects can have many kinds of semantic relationships.

1. 宾语是动作的受事。

The object may be the patient of the action.

吃苹果　送人　挂衣服

同意结婚　广播新闻

2. 宾语是动作的施事。

The object may be the agent of the action.

住人　来客人了　死了丈夫

门口站着一个人

3. 宾语是动作的工具。

The object may be the instrument used in the action.

洗冷水　吹风　打针

骑马　　装箱子

4. 宾语是动作产生的结果。

The object may be the result produced by the action.

写信　　照相　　煮饭

写东西　　盖房子　　打毛衣

5. 宾语是动作的处所。

The object may be the location of the action.

住北大　　去上海　　进门

过桥　　下楼

6. 宾语表示动作的时间。

The object may indicate the time of the action.

等了一会儿　　去了一个月

住三天

7. 宾语表示的是数量。

The object may be a numeral measure word.

买了两斤　　看了几页

借了五本　　盖了三间

8. 宾语表示主语的类别。

The object may show the type of the subject.

鲸鱼属于哺乳动物。

他们几个是一个小组。

9. 宾语表示复指。

The object may refer back to the subject.

你只能怪自己。

烟还是戒了它吧!

小王你就别叫他了。

述语主要由及物动词以及由及物动词组成的动词性结构充当。例如：

The main component of the predicate is usually a transitive verb or a verb construction formed with a transitive verb. For example:

看书　　听音乐　　参观工厂

看不看电影　　不同意去

助动词也能带宾语。例如：

Auxiliary verbs may also take objects. For example:

能学好　　应该去　　愿意帮助人

宾语主要由名词、代词或名词性结构充当。例如：

Object may be nouns, pronouns or nominal structures. For example:

喝汽水　　吃冰棍　　上课

写什么　　问谁　　上哪儿

买两本　　要红颜色　　记住别人说的

动词、形容词和由它们组成的词组也能作宾语。例如：

Verbs, adjectives or phrases composed of them may also be object.

动＋动：喜欢笑　学游泳　受折磨

动＋形：爱干净　怕冷　放晴

动＋动宾：学养花　反对说空话　喜欢骑马

动＋主谓：同意我参加　相信明天会下雨

发现自己做错了

动＋偏正：想早点走　决定立刻动手术

商量怎么办

动＋动补：发现走远了　听说喝醉了

动词后附“到、在、向、于”等介词可以带时间词、处所词作宾语。例如：

Prepositions 到，在，向，and 于 after verbs can take time words or location words to act as objects.

等到天亮　走到车站

住在北京　挂在墙上　发生在九月

来自上海　出自内心

走向未来　奔向前方

产于青海　生于一九五六年

这里看成动补结构带宾语，因为补语只限于谓词性成分，而且介词之后可以有停顿，可以插入“了”。

Here it is considered as verb-complement structure taking an object, because only predicative elements can act as complements. Besides, there may be a pause after the preposition and 了 may be inserted.

住在北京

述　宾

述补

二、几种主要的宾语类型　Major types of objects

（一）施事宾语　The agent as object

主语不一定是施事，宾语也不一定是受事。在“信写完了”中，“信”是“写”的对象，是受事，在句中作主语。在“来客人了”中，“客人”是“来”的主动者,是施事,在句中作宾语。在“这间屋子住四个人”中,“屋子”是处所主语,“四个人”是施事宾语。

The subject is not always the agent, nor is the object necessarily the patient. In 信写完了,信 is the object of 写, the recipient. It's the subject of the sentence. In 来客人了,客人 is the agent of 来, it's the object of the sentence. In 这间屋子住四个人,屋子 is the subject relating to location. 四个人 is the agent as object.

主语和宾语是句法概念,施事和受事是语义概念。我们不能把受事主语理解为宾语提前,也不能把施事宾语理解为主语后置,因为还原以后的句子的意思和原来不一样。例如:

Subject and object are syntactic concepts; agent and patient are semantic concepts. We cannot interpret a patient subject as a preposed object, nor can we explain an agent object as a delayed subject. If such a rearrangement is done, the original meaning is changed. For Example:

一锅饭吃不了十个人。(指锅小,饭不够十个人吃)

十个人吃不了一锅饭。(指锅大饭多,十个人吃不了)

施事宾语的特点 Characteristics of the agent as object:

1. 宾语是无定的。

The object is indefinite.

屋里坐满了人。

胡同里走来一个人。

摩托车上骑着一男一女。

2. 述语成分是个复杂形式。

The predicate is complex.

月台上站满了旅客。

空中飞来几只天鹅。

船上下去几个人。

(二) 处所宾语 Location object

处所宾语表示动作行为的处所或运动的起止点。

Location object refers to the location of the action or the starting or ending spot of the action.

1. 宾语说明动作的位置。

The object indicates th place of the action.

他坐在桥上。

他跪在地上。

他站在院子里。

2. 宾语说明被安置的地方。

The object indicates where something has been placed.

书搁书架上。

花瓶摆在茶几上。

礼物放在桌上。

3. 宾语说明运动的起止点。

The object indicates the starting or ending spot of the action.

我明天回上海。

他明天离开北京。

述语后不用介词,直接带处所宾语是汉语的一个特点。例如:

No preposition is used after the verb. The direct use of the locative object after the verb is a unique feature of Chinese.

Examples:

我住校外。

他站门口。

箱子放地上。

书放包里。

(三) 准宾语　Quasi-object

由名词、代词等充当的一般宾语是真宾语，而由动量和时量结构充任的宾语或人称代词加"的""什么"充任的非实指宾语叫准宾语。准宾语大致有四类：

When nouns, pronouns act as objects, the objects are true objects; when verb-numeral, time-numeral structures, or personal pronoun plus 的 or 什么 act as objects, the objects are called quasi-objects. There are four types of quasi-object:

1. 由表示动量和时量的数量词构成的。

Formed by numeral measure word indicating action or time.

动量		时量	
	打了一下		等了三天
	看了三次		看了一会儿
	去了两回		走了一个月
	踢了一脚		休息了两个星期

2. 由指人的名词或代词+"的"充任非实指宾语。

Nouns referring to people or pronouns + 的 employed as quasi-objects.

听老师的，没错。

你干你的，怕什么。

他说他的，你干你的。

3. 由"什么"充任虚指宾语(大多表示否定意义)。

什么 as a false object (mostly expressing negation).

你还看什么，走吧。

你知道什么。

你哭什么。

4. 由"它"充当虚指宾语。

它 as a false object.

唱它一段(京剧)。

尝它一口。

听它一句。

管他三七二十一。

(四) 双宾语 Double objects

一个动词后带有两个宾语的叫双宾语。靠近动词的指人的宾语叫间接宾语,远离动词的指事物的宾语叫直接宾语。

When a verb takes two objects, they are called double objects. The one closest to the verb which indicates a person is the indirect object. The one which is farther from the verb indicating an inanimate object is the direct object.

从结构分析,双宾语可以看作是述宾结构带宾语。例如:

Analyzing from structure, double objects can be considered as a verb-object construction taking an object.

给他书	告诉你一个好消息
述 宾	述 宾
述宾	述 宾

双宾语中两个宾语可以都是真宾语,也可以是一真一准。

两个宾语都是真宾语的,表示的意义有三种:

With double objects, both may be true objects or one may be true and the other quasi-object. There are three meanings which can be expressed when both objects are true objects.

1. 表示给予 Conferring (giving):

给他一本书。

送你两张电影票。

还你十块钱。

告诉你一个好消息。

2. 表示取得 Acquisition:

买了他一所房子。

拿了他一件东西。

收到他一封信。

问你一个问题。

3. 表示等同 Equivalency:

叫他小王。

你别叫我先生。

当他自己人。

骂他废物。

有的双宾语之间有领属关系,变成了单宾语。例如:

Some double objects show possession and could be treated as a single object.

A. 借了他(的)一支笔。

B. 租了他(的)一间屋。

C. 收到他(的)一封信。

D. 拿了他(的)一本书。

A和B句的动词“借”和“租”如果表示“给予”意义,那么“他”是间接宾语;如果表示“取得”意义,那么“他”表示领属。C句和D句都是单宾语,“他”表示领属。

If the verbs 借 and 租 in A and B express the idea of conferring, then 他 is indirect object; but if they express the idea of acquisition, then 他 shows possession. Both C and D have single object: 他 shows possession.

双宾语如果是一个真宾语,一个准宾语,其位置如下:

If one object is a true object and the other quasi-object, their positions are as follows:

1．真宾语＋准宾语

The true object followed by the quasi-object.

等他一会儿。

喊了小王几声。

拍了他一下。

你劝他几句。

他该你多少？

2．准宾语＋真宾语

The quasi-object followed by the true object.

下一会儿棋。

换一换衣服。

等一会儿小王。

有的动量词和名词构成偏正结构，动量词相当于名量词，这时宾语变成单宾语。这可以通过变换看出来。例如：

Sometimes the verbal measure word combines with a noun to form an endocentric construction, the verbal measure word corresponds to a noun measure word. In this case, the object is considered a single object.

进了一次城。 ⟶ 一次城也没进过。

看了两回京剧。 ⟶ 一回京剧也没看过。

请了一次客。 ⟶ 一次客也没请过。

住了两星期医院。⟶ 一次医院也没住过。

请了三天假。 ⟶ 一天假也没请过。

练　习

一、按下列要求举例(每种举两个)：

1. 施事宾语
2. 受事宾语
3. 工具宾语
4. 结果宾语
5. 处所宾语
6. 时间宾语
7. 数量宾语

二、仿例指出下列宾语所表示的语法意义：

修自行车	看书	(对象或受事宾语)
骑马	乘飞机	(　　　　　　)
做菜	打毛衣	(　　　　　　)
照两张	喝二两	(　　　　　　)
走了半个月	休息几分钟	(　　　　　　)
开船	卸车	(　　　　　　)
来车了	走人	(　　　　　　)
上北京	下江南	(　　　　　　)
前面有人	水里有鱼	(　　　　　　)
听音乐	打网球	(　　　　　　)
养花	做家具	(　　　　　　)
出国	进城	(　　　　　　)
来过几次	放了两枪	(　　　　　　)
作报告	修改文章	(　　　　　　)

熊猫属熊科　　　他俩是一班的(　　　　　　　)
你只能靠自己　　书还是买了它(　　　　　　　)

三、指出下列句子中的错误并改正:

1. 怕困难是失败的保证。
2. 大家都为建设国家作出自己的力量。
3. 他的行动感动了人们的心情。
4. 他总算找到了工厂的下落。
5. 我想推辞他的礼物。
6. 他很称心自己的工作。

第五节　述语和补语

Verbs and Complement

述补结构里的述语表示的是动作、行为和性质,补语说明动作的结果或状态。

述语一般由单个的动词或形容词充当。补语一般由动词、形容词、副词等充当。

The verb in a verb-complement structure expresses action, behavior or character; the complement indicates the result of the action or state.

Usually the verb slot is filled by a simple verb or an adjective, the complement slot is usually filled by verbs, adjectives, adverbs.

补语和宾语的区别在于宾语可以由名词性成分充当也可以由谓词性成分充当,而补语只能由谓语性成分充当。

The difference between a complement and an object is that the object may be a nominal element or a predicative element, while the complement can only be a predicative element.

述宾:买票　　　送礼物　　听报告

　　喜欢骑马　决定出国　承认这是事实

述补:听懂　　　洗干净　　拿回来

　　唱得好　　热得很　　说得大家笑了

根据补语对述语补充说明的情况,大致可以把补语分为四类:结果补语、趋向补语、可能补语和程度补语。

We can identify four types of complements according to their meanings: resultative, directional, potential, and degree.

一、结果补语 Resultative complements

表示动作或变化所产生的结果的补语叫结果补语。这类补语和前边的动词结合得很紧。

Complements which indicate the result caused by action or changes are resultative complements.

This type of complement has a very close relationship with the preceding verb.

动+动:看见　听懂　学会　说完

　　拿走　打破　杀死　用光

动+形:变大　走远　拉长　吃饱

　　抓紧　写好　说清楚

能充当结果补语的动词不多。常见的有"走、跑、动、翻、病、死、懂、成、完、通、穿、倒、透"等。

Not many verbs can be resultative complements. The most common are 走,跑,动,翻,病,死,懂,成,完,通,穿,倒,透,etc.

带结果补语的动补结构在语法功能上相当于一个动词。它们之间的区别在于动补结构可以用“得”“不”扩展,而复合词不能。

The verb-complement structure taking a resultative complement corresponds to a verb in terms of grammatical function. The difference is that verb-complement structure can be expanded by using 得 and 不, while a compound word cannot.

带结果补语的动补结构的特点 Characteristics of resultative complements:

1. 后面可以带动词后缀“了”“过”。

May take verb suffixes 了 and 过.

学会了　看见过　听懂了　喝醉过

2. 后边还可以带宾语。

May take an object.

学会了开车　看见过大海　喝醉过酒

听懂了京剧　笑破了肚皮　接通了电话

3. 补语是形容词的结果补语多指不如意的。

When the resultative complement is an adjective, it usually indicates dissatisfaction.

鞋买小了　房子盖高了　体重减轻了

衣服裁短了　我吃多了　你来晚了

汤做咸了　车开快了有危险

4. 否定形式是在述补结构前头加“没(有)”。如果用“不”否定,后边往往有别的话。

The negative form 没有 is placed in front of the verb complement structure. When 不 is used for negation, there is usually an additional phrase after the complement.

没(有)听懂　没(有)写好　没(有)拿走

不学会怎么行呢?
不吃饱会饿的。
}表示条件

二、趋向补语　Directional complement

由趋向动词"来、去、进、出、上、下、回、过、起"等充任的补语叫趋向补语。

Complements which use the directional verbs 来,去,进,出,上,下,回,过,起 are called directional complements.

拿来　送去　走进　跑出　爬上

跳下　寄回　飞过　抓起

汉语里的趋向动词总共有二十二个,分三小类:

There are 22 directional verbs in Chinese and they can be divided into three types:

1. "来、去"两个表示趋向,以说话人的位置为准。

来 and 去 show directions toward or away from the speaker.

2. "上、下、进、出、回、过、起"表示趋向,以运动事物原来的位置为准。

上,下,进,出,回,过,and 起 show directions of moving object from its original spot.

3. "上来、下来、进来、出来、回来、过来、起来、上去、下去、进去、出去、回去、过去"表示的方向和说话人的位置有关,也跟事物原来的位置有关。

The directions expressed by these words are concerned with both the speaker's place and the original place of the object.

1 \ 3 \ 2	上	下	进	出	回	过	起
来	上来	下来	进来	出来	回来	过来	起来
去	上去	下去	进去	出去	回去	过去	—

由"来、去"充任补语的述补结构后边只能带一般宾语,不能带处所宾语。处所宾语要插在动补之间。例如:

Verb-complement structures using 来 and 去 may be followed only by an ordinary object, not an object of location. Objects of location must be inserted between the verb and complement.

For example:

送来一封信　　拿去一本书　　寄来一百元

* 送来学校　　* 拿去宿舍　　* 寄来北京

送学校来　　拿宿舍去　　寄北京来

但是由"上、下、进、出、回、过"等动词作补语的述补结构后面可以带处所宾语。例如:

But the structures which employ the verbs 上,下,进,出,回,过 as complements may have an object of location following the verb-complement. For example:

走进教室　爬上香山

搬回宿舍　借出图书馆

第三小类中的"进来、进去、上来、上去、回来、回去"等又可以放在别的动词后边作复合趋向补语。例如:

进来,进去,上来,上去,回来,回去 of the third type may be used after other verbs to form complex directional complement. For example:

走进来　跑出来　爬上来　跳下来

送回来　拿过来　站起来　—

走进去　跑出去　爬上去　跳下去

送回去　拿过去　—　—

带复合趋向补语的述补结构所带宾语的位置有两种情况：

There are two possible placement slots for the objects of verb complement structures with complex directional complements:

1. 一般宾语的位置比较自由；处所宾语只能插在复合趋向补语中间。

Most objects are free in terms of placement, but objects of location must be placed in the middle of the complex directional complement.

走进教室里来

拿出楼去

爬上山顶去

跳下水去

送回家去

飞过大海去

2. 宾语是无定的位置其比宾语是有定的自由。

Objects which are indefinite have more flexibility than objects which are definite.

无定宾语的位置有三种情况：

There are three positions for indefinite objects:

拿出一本书来（补语中间 between the complements）

拿出来一本书（补语之后 after the complement）

拿一本书出来（补语之前 before the complement）

有定宾语的位置只有一种情况：

Positioning of definite objects has only one possibility:

拿出那本书来

* 拿出来那本书

* 拿那本书出来

趋向补语还有引申的用法:

Directional complements have extended usage:

下	下去	出来	起来
坐得下	说下去	说出来	唱起来
吃得下	做下去	听出来	笑起来
放得下	住下去	看出来	收起来
(有地方容纳)	(动作继续)	(趋向不具体)	(动作开始)

三、可能补语　Potential complements

表示可能性的述补结构中的补语叫可能补语。例如:

Verb-complement structures which express potentiality are called potential complements.

肯定形式		否定形式
看得见	(能看见)	看不见
写得完	(能写完)	写不完
说得清楚	(能说清楚)	说不清楚
进得去	(能进去)	进不去
拿得出来	(能拿出来)	拿不出来

大部分结果补语和趋向补语都能转换成可能补语。例如:

Most resultative and directional complements can be converted into potential complements.

说清楚——说得清楚/说不清楚

学会——学得会/学不会

放上去——放得上去/放不上去

拿出来——拿得出来/拿不出来

宾语的位置总是在整个述补结构的后头。例如：

An object will always come at the end of the verb-complement structure.

看得见人

叫不出名字

拿得出来一千块钱

爬不上去那座山

还有两种比较固定的可能补语：

There are two other kinds of regular potential complements.

一种是"X得"式　One is in form of X得：

看得/看不得

吃得/吃不得

去得/去不得

动得/动不得

特点　Characteristics：

1. 对动作本身能否进行作出判断。

Indicates a judgement on whether or not the action itself is possible.

这些水果是蜡做的，看得吃不得。

2. 主语一般是受事。

The subject is usually the patient.

这个电影小孩子看不得。

3. 多用否定式,用肯定形式时大多与否定形式对举出现。

Usually used in the negative form. When used in positive, it's generally paralleled with negative form.

这种事反对不得。

他的话相信不得。

不管去得去不得,我今天一定要去。

某些形容词谓语带可能补语,多是否定式。

Some adjective predicates taking potential complements are normally negative.

乱不得　　马虎不得

快不得　　着急不得

热不得　　大意不得

另一种是“X 得了”式　The other is in form of X 得了:

走得了/走不了

办得了/办不了

拿得了/拿不了

完成得了/完成不了

特点　Characteristics:

1. 多指主观上能不能。

Mostly a subjective comment of possibility.

2. 主语是施事。

The subject is the agent.

3. 肯定式否定式都用。

Used in both positive and negative forms.

决定得了/决定不了

接受得了/接受不了

四、程度补语 Complement of degree

表示动作或性质的程度的述补结构中的补语叫程度补语。

The complement in the verb-complement structure which indicates the degree of the action or characteristic is called complement of degree.

程度补语有三种形式：

There are three forms of complement of degree:

1. 带"得"式 Using 得：

唱得好	唱得很好	白得像雪
洗得干净	洗得挺干净	红得发紫
写得手发麻	写得手都麻了	冷得发抖
听得呆了	说得大家笑了	热得很
气得脸白了	急得直出汗	闷得慌
暖和得不得了	争论得面红耳赤	

这种结构里的述语是动词或形容词，时态既可以表示已然，也可以表示未然。

The 述语 in this form is a verb or an adjective. The tense may be past or future.

2. 带"个"式 Using 个：

说个清楚 问个明白 玩个痛快

说了个一清二楚 撕了个粉碎 围了个水泄不通

说个没完 下个不停 哭个不止 争个没完没了

这种结构里的述语限于动词，时态既可表示未然，又可表示已然。

The 述语 in this form can only be a verb. It can still express future or past.

3. 带“了”式　Using 了:

好极了　坏极了　热极了　冷极了

恨透了　坏透了　讨厌透了

香死了　臭死了　辣死了　脏死了

气坏了　累坏了　急坏了

这种结构里的补语表示程度高，一般没有否定式。某些表示心理感觉的(如“透了”“死了”“坏了”)中间可插“我”“他”“人”等。

The complement in this form shows a high degree. There is usually no negative form. In the middle of some words which express emotion (e.g. 透了，死了，坏了)我，他，人，etc. can be inserted.

程度补语和可能补语的区别:

Comparison between complement of degree and potential complement:

	程度补语	可能补语
扩展	唱得(很)好(极了)	—
否定式	唱得不好	唱不好
补语成分	洗得干净	洗得掉/干净
宾语	—	看得见黑板上的字
重音	洗得 ′干净	′洗得干净
提问方式	唱得好不好?	唱得好唱不好?

练　习

一、在句中动词后填上适当的结果补语：

1. 这本字典很有用，你要想办法买(　　)它。
2. 要想办(　　)一件事，不下功夫是不行的。
3. 他出来不到一个月，带来的钱都用(　　)了。
4. 一个上午，他写(　　)了三封信。
5. 这里的电话真难打，打了半天才打(　　)。
6. 如果柿子是软的，那就熟(　　)了。
7. 这酒不能再喝了，再喝会喝(　　)的。
8. 他什么也没学(　　)，就学(　　)了吹牛。
9. 不到半年时间，他几乎跑(　　)了整个中国。
10. 由于天气不好，我的旅行计划全打(　　)了。
11. 学过的东西要抓(　　)复习，不然就忘了。
12. 人到(　　)了就开车。
13. 听说孩子丢了，母亲急(　　)了。
14. 鸡蛋煮的时间长了就煮(　　)了。
15. 病人救(　　)了，大夫却累(　　)了。
16. 由于我看(　　)了时间，没赶上火车。
17. 这种菜我已经吃(　　)了，不爱吃了。
18. 进了商店，眼睛都看(　　)了，不知道买什么好。

二、在各句空白处填上适当的趋向补语：

1. 他说______了我们的心里话。
2. 你把我的电话号码记______。
3. 他的文章在报上登______了。

4. 那辆出租车从我们面前开______了。

5. 看______，今天会下雨。

6. 这间屋子里能放______几张床？

7. 我们已经住______了新楼。

8. 当他醒______的时候，才发现自己躺在医院里。

9. 这个手提包看______不大，装的东西可不少。

10. 请你帮我把行李搬______船______。

三、在括号里填上适当的趋向补语：

1. 汽车停______了，从车里出______两个人。

2. 太阳从东方升______了。

3. 信已经寄______三天了。

4. 他是上个月从英国______的。

5. 你把药喝______，病就会好的。

6. 他把箱子拿______屋里，走______屋子，锁______门。

7. 飞机从人们头顶上飞______了。

8. 昨天夜里，他想______想______还是决定去。

9. 你回______，我有话对你说。

10. 对方送______的礼物，他欣然接受______了。

11. 像他这种人，能干______什么好事______呢！

12. 听到呼救声，他衣服也没脱就跳______水______。

13. 快跑！后面的人追______了。

14. 他爬______树顶，摸了两个鸟蛋______。

15. 请拿______证件______。

16. 他随手拿______一张报纸看了______。

17. 不管有多大困难，你都要坚持______。

18. 你敢从这座独木桥上走______吗？

四、改正下列各句中的错误：

1. 外面下雪起来。

2. 我想他的名字起来。

3. 火箭飞上去天了。

4. 下课以后,大家都回去宿舍。

5. 农民的生活一天天好下去。

6. 他走进去门里。

五、选择适当的可能补语填空:

1. 这种药有副作用,吃不______。(了、得、完)

2. 我说的话,他一点也听不______。(下去、起来、进去)

3. 那样的东西,谁能买得______?(起、下、了)

4. 你别听他的,他的话相信不______。(下去、了、得)

5. 这些水果都是假的,看得吃不______。(了、得、下)

6. 你别看不______他,他很有学问。(得、起、上)

7. 做作业要认真,马虎不______。(了、上、得)

8. 我想丢了的东西很难找得______。(来、着、回)

9. 我送给他的礼物,他一点也看不______。(起、下、上)

10. 他这个人,简直是老虎的屁股摸不______。(得、了、着)

六、把下列句子改成可能补语:

1. 九月中能开学。

2. 九月中他不能回来。

3. 菜太多了,没法吃完。

4. 他累了,不能走了。

5. 这箱子太重,一个人没法搬。

6. 他的风筝不能飞。

7. 他声音很小,我们都没听见。

8. 七天不吃饭,人能饿死吗?

9. 表丢了,还能找到吗?

10. 我打了几次电话都没打通。

11. 京剧一般人不能听懂。

12. 没有钥匙我不能进屋。
13. 他网球打得那么好,我怎么能打败他呢?
14. 没有飞机,我们不能走了。
15. 他感冒了,头很疼,不能上课。
16. 皮大衣那么贵,谁有钱买?
17. 有的电影小孩子不能看。
18. 我不知道我能不能考上研究生。

七、举例说明程度补语和可能补语的不同。

第六节　定语和状语
Attributives and Adverbials

一、修饰语和中心语　Qualifier and head word

偏正结构由中心语和修饰语两部分组成。修饰语在前,中心语在后。中心语是整个偏正结构的核心。修饰语的语法意义在于限制和描写中心语。

修饰语和中心语在意义上的联系是多种多样的,基本上可分为两类:

An endocentric construction is composed of a head word and a qualifier. The qualifier comes before the head word. The head word is the central part of the endocentric construction. The grammatical significance of the qualifier is that it limits or describes the head word.

There are many types of semantic relationships between the qualifier and the head word, but basically they can be divided into two types:

1. 名词性偏正结构(中心语是名词性的,整个偏正结构也是名词性的)

Nominal endocentric construction(the head word is a noun and the endocentric construction itself is nominal).

木头桌子　塑料雨伞

(名+名)　(质料 material)

我们的大学　他的汽车

(代+名)　(领属 possession)

三个人　很多树

(数量+名)　(数量 quantity)

昨天的报纸　北京的秋天

(时间/处所+名 time/location+noun)

新书　高高的山

(形+名)　(性状 property)

喝水的杯子　理发的剪刀

(动+名)　(用途 usage)

这类结构一般在句中不能作谓语,修饰语叫定语。

This type of construction may not serve as the predicate in a sentence. The qualifier is called an attributive.

2. 谓词性偏正结构(中心语是动词、形容词,整个偏正结构是谓词性的)

Verbal endocentric constructions (the head word is a verb or an adjective; the endocentric construction is verbal).

快走　仔细想　(形+动)　(方式 way)

小聪明	飞快	(形+形)	(性状 property)
很简单	更重要	(副+形)	(程度 degree)
应该去	必须注意	(助+动)	(意愿 will)

这类结构在句中作谓语,修饰语叫状语。

This type of construction may be the predicate in a sentence. The qualifier is called an adverbial.

二、定语和状语的区分 The difference between attributives and adverbials

人们通常总以为名词前的修饰语是定语,动词、形容词前的修饰语是状语,但事实并非都如此。

我们不能只根据中心语的性质(是名词还是动词、形容词)来确定修饰语是定语还是状语。也就是说,名词前的修饰语不一定是定语,动词、形容词前的修饰语不一定是状语。例如:

It is generally believed that the qualifiers of nouns were attributives and the qualifiers of verbs or adjectives were adverbials. This is not necessarily always true.

We cannot define the qualifier as attributive or adverbial based only on the character of the head word—whether it is a noun, a verb, or an adjective). In other words, the qualifier preceding a noun is not always an attributive; a qualifier preceding a verb or adjective is not always an adverbial.

For example:

A组	B组
(今天)刚星期二。	(感谢)大家的支持。
(他)已经大学生了。	(得到)他的同意。

就五个人。　　　　　　　　（记住）血的教训。

都十二点了。　　　　　　　（懂得）太阳的伟大。

区别:

A组:(1)副+名(数量);(2)作谓语;(3)修饰语是状语。

B组:(1)名(代)+动/形;(2)不能作谓语;(3)修饰语是定语。

区分定语还是状语,既要看中心语,又要看修饰语,还要看整个偏正结构是名词性的还是谓词性的。

To distinguish between attributives and adverbials, it is necessary to consider both the head word and the qualifier and whether the entire endocentric construction is nominal or verbal.

三、作定语的成分　Components of attributives

(一) 名词、形容词、代词、数量词都可以作定语

Nouns, adjectives, pronouns, and numeral measure word all can serve as attributives. For example:

1. 名词作定语　Nouns as attributive

带"的"不带"的"有三种情况:

Nouns with or without 的 as attributives have three cases:

(1) 可带"的"可不带"的":

With or without 的, the meaning remains unchanged:

木头房子　木头的房子

中国历史　中国的历史

北京大学学生　北京大学的学生

(2) 一定带"的":

的 must be added:

水的成分　书的内容　鞋的质量

人的寿命　花的颜色　球的形状

(3) 带不带"的"意思不一样：

The meanings are different with or without 的：

A组 Group A	B组 Group B
中国的客人	中国客人
(外国人 foreigner)	(中国人 Chinese)
孩子的脾气	孩子脾气
(指孩子的 refers to kids)	(指大人的 refers to adults)
狐狸的尾巴	狐狸尾巴
(实指 actual reference)	(比喻用法 metaphorical)
木头的人	木头人
(木制人 wooden figure)	(像木头 like wood)
烟的味儿	烟味儿

A组表领属关系,B组表示属性,有的有比况意味。

Group A shows possession, while group B indicates nature or comparison.

2. 形容词作定语　Adjectives as attributives

新书　　高楼　　好人

干净的衣服　　漂亮的城市　　聪明的孩子

(1) 单音节形容词作定语比较自由,但有选择。

Monosyllabic adjectives which act as attributives are quite flexible. Examples:

香花	* 香饭	香喷喷的饭
薄纸	* 薄雪	薄薄的雪

凉水　　　* 凉手　　冰凉的手

脏衣服　　* 脏糖　　脏里呱叽的糖

蓝墨水　　* 蓝天空　蓝蓝的天空

(2) 双音节形容词作定语不自由，加“的”的比不加“的”的普遍。

Disyllabic adjectives which serve as attributives are not flexible. Those followed by 的 are more common than those not followed by 的.

勇敢的士兵　　* 勇敢士兵

美丽的公园　　* 美丽公园

清洁的房间　　* 清洁房间

方便的交通　　* 方便交通

客气的态度　　* 客气态度

3. 代词作定语　Pronouns as adjectives

我哥哥　　我的哥哥

他母亲　　他的母亲

我们老师　我们的老师

* 谁书　　谁的书

哪个人　　* 哪个的人

什么颜色　* 什么的颜色

(1) 表示亲属或领属的，带“的”不带“的”的都可以。表示一般事物的单说时必须带“的”。

When expressing possession or kinship 的 is not indispensable; when expressing ordinary things, 的 is needed.

我的眼镜

他的自行车

(2) 代词“这、那、哪”+量词,可以直接作定语。

Pronoun 这,那,哪 + measure word can be attributives directly.

这本书

那本小说

哪个孩子

(3) 表示领属的必须带“的”。

的 is needed when expressing possession.

这间的主人不在家。

哪个的孩子。

谁的孩子。

4. 数量词作定语 Numeral measure word as attributives

(1) 表示限制。直接作定语,不带“的”。

Showing restriction, can be attributives without 的.

我买了五斤橘子。

我买了三本书。

我买了两张电影票。

(2) 表示描写。有时带“的”有时不带“的”。

Showing description,的 can be added or left out.

他买了一条三斤重的鱼。

他买了三十斤橘子。

他是六十岁的老人。

她有三个孩子。

(3) 借用名词作量词。可以用“的”。

Using nouns as measure words,的 can be used.

一鼻子的灰　　一身的水

一手的油　　一头的汗

（二）动词或动词结构作定语

Verbs or verb constructions as attributives

买的纸	看的画	出租汽车
订的合同	吃的水果	研究方法
提的意见	参观的人	营业时间

不能名词化的双音节动词不能直接作定语。例如：

Disyllabic verbs which cannot be nominalized cannot directly serve as attributives.

喜欢的东西	打听的消息
盼望的事情	修理的汽车

各种动词结构作定语的情况 Verbal constructions used as attributives:

写好的信	(动补 verb complement)
虚心学习的人	(偏正 endocentric)
上课的人	(述宾 verb object)
要完成的任务	(偏正 endocentric)
从欧洲来的学生	(偏正 endocentric)
去参观的同学	(连动 linked verbs)
讨论研究的题目	(并列 coordinative)
他没去的原因	(主谓 subject predicate)

四、定语的次序 Order in attributive

1．带"的"的定语在不带"的"的定语之前。

An attributive with 的 precedes an attributive without 的.

玻璃的小茶杯　　　　漂亮的新衣服

电动的小玩具　　　　他的汉语词典

如果是数量词或领属性成分作定语属组合式偏正结构，只能前置。

If the attributive is served by a numeral measure word or elements showing possession, then, it is a compound endocentric structure and can only be put ahead.

一套三居室的房子　　一封没打开的信

他最大的孩子　　　　世界最高的山

2. 如果几个定语都不带"的"，一般次序是：领属性定语 + 数量词 + 形容词 + 名词 + 中心语。

If none of several attributives has 的, the order is generally as follows:

Possessive + numeral measure word + adjective + noun + head word

他　那件　新　皮　大衣

注意　Note:

(1) 数量、指代之间可前可后。

Numeral measure words and demonstratives may be placed ahead or after.

{最大的一间办公室
{一间最大的办公室

{穿西装的那个青年
{那个穿西装的青年

(2) 如果修饰语本身又是个偏正结构，就不能一层一层去分析，而要根据结合的程度分层。

If the qualifier itself is an endocentric construction then the analysis cannot be done level by level. The levels are determined by the degree of linkage or combination.

新同学的宿舍　同学的新宿舍

“新同学的宿舍”不是“新宿舍”扩展来的。

新同学的宿舍 is not extended from 新宿舍 .

五、作状语的成分　Elements which can be adverbials

作状语的成分不仅仅限于副词,形容词等也能作状语,不过不太自由。

Adverbs are not the only elements which can be adverbials; adjectives can also be adverbials but they are less flexible.

1. 副词作状语　Adverbs as adverbials

很重要　好漂亮

刚来　忽然不见了

2. 形容词作状语(大部分形容词不能作状语)　Adjectives as adverbials (most adjectives may not serve as adverbials)

轻放　慢走　高喊　快跑

(单音节形容词不自由　monosyllabic adjectives are less flexible)

仔细听　老实说　热烈欢迎　努力工作

(双音节形容词　disyllabic adjective)

仔细地看　勉强地笑笑　公开地解释　严肃地指出　(双音节形容词 disyllabic adjective)

慢慢地来　好好地说　深深地吸了口气　满满

地倒了一杯酒　　（重叠式 repetition）

3. 介词结构作状语　Prepositional phrases as adverbials

为人民服务　把书拿来　在湖边散步

向他问好　对人和气　到上海出差

4. 动量词作状语　Verbal measure words as adverbials

一次没去　一把拉住　一口吞下

一眼看去　一遍也没看过

5. 其他作状语的成分　Other elements as adverbials

联合结构（比况性的）　Compound structure:

没完没了地说

你一句我一句地讨论

人不知鬼不觉地溜走了

东张张西望望地到处乱看

名 + 地（+ V）　Noun + 地（+ V）:

科学地总结过去的经验

任务历史地落在我们头上

他的手本能地缩了回来

有（无）+ 宾 + 地（+ V）　有（无）+ object + 地（+ V）:

有组织地参观

无目的地旅行

无代价地提供援助

代词　Pronoun:

他哪儿来的钱？

你怎么不找个工作做？

数量词　Numeral measure word:

他想一口吃个胖子

三天看完一本书

六、状语的次序 Order in adverbials

状语的次序比定语的次序自由。多层状语的一般顺序是：

More flexible than attributives, the order of multi-level adverbials is as follows:

(1) 表示时间的名词或介词结构；(2) 表示处所的名词或介词结构；(3) 副词(有时在第二项前)；(4) 形容词或动词。例如：

①Nouns or prepositional phrases which express time ②Nouns or prepositional phrases of location ③Adverbs (sometimes come before the second item) ④Adjectives or verbs.

Examples:

我昨天在图书馆里又仔细地翻了一遍。

你明天下午在校门口等我。

他们每个星期六晚上在饭厅举行舞会。

他轻轻地从桌上拿起书包走出房间。

这件事很容易办。

练　习

一、按照定语的次序连成句子：

1. 那　钢琴　特制的　一架　是　星海牌　国产
2. 她家　李庄　住在　小院里　村东头的
3. 北大　综合　一所　全国　文理　重点　是　大学

4. 财产　是　唯一的　手杖　一根　他　木制　不离手的

5. 她　牺牲的　是　女连长　唯一的　在小树林战斗中

6. 我　精心　买了　制作的　大蛋糕　用九种材料　一盒

7. 那座　塔　叫　什么名字　立在湖边的　高十三层的

8. 她　一件　兰底白花　穿　连衣裙　短袖　柔姿纱

9. 李立　是　走在前面的　穿夹克衫的　中等身材的　那个人　我们班的

10. 他　一幅　水彩画　象征丰收的　画了

二、按照状语的次序连词成句：

1. 他　里里外外　一遍　把屋子　打扫了　彻底

2. 他　一字不差地　能　几乎　许多　古文　熟练地　背下　诗词　和

3. 张老师　一句一句地　很　教　我们　耐心地　说中文

4. 他　按时　下午四点半　开到　把车　每天　十字路口

5. 我　玩了　公园　一个下午　昨天　到　跟朋友

6. 我　跑三圈　沿着　和同屋　勺园楼　每天早上

7. 树叶　落在　微风　随着　轻轻地　地上　一片片地

8. 汽车　滑动　慢慢　向前　在人流中　一点一点地

9. 我　摔倒　连人带马　不小心　在马路上

10. 他　有礼貌地　向客人　很　说了声　再见

三、把下列各组句子改写成一个包括多项状语的句子：

1. 孩子们向公园走去。
   孩子们兴高采烈地走去。
   孩子们昨天下午走了。

2. 他已经回国了。
   他上个星期回国了。
   他跟他朋友一起回国了。

3. 我的同屋对我说:“今晚有杂技演出。”
我的同屋高兴地说:“今晚有杂技演出。”
我的同屋中午说:“今晚有杂技演出。”

4. 你现在通知他一声。
你赶快通知他一声。
你必须通知他一声。

5. 他每天下午打网球。
他在楼前打网球。
他同小李打网球。

第四章　几种特殊的句法结构
Chapter Four　Several Unique Syntactic Structures

第一节　复谓结构
Double Predicative Constructions

先重温五种结构类型：

First let's review the five types of structures:

下棋打扑克　刮风下雨　（联合 compound）

喜欢打网球　希望他回来（述宾 verb object）

搬下船去　气得哭了　（述补 verb complement）

学习历史很重要　走路要当心

（主谓 subject predicate）

仔细检查一下　勉强笑了笑

（偏正 endocentric）

再看下面六个句子：

Have a look at the following six sentences:

出去打电话

想办法解决

我请他来我家作客

叫他出来

他越说越激动

我一看就明白

显然,这六句不同于前五种基本句法结构。

Obviously these six types are not the same as the other five basic syntactic constructions.

由两个或两个以上的谓词或谓词性结构组成的结构叫复谓结构。它不只是作谓语,还可以作其他句子成分。例如:

Constructions composed of two or more predicates or predicative structures are called double predicative constructions. They can serve not only as predicates but may also fill other sentence slots.

For example:

他们去南极考察。	(作谓语 predicate)
去南极考察一定很有意思。	(作主语 subject)
他们打算去南极考察。	(作宾语 object)
去南极考察的人都回来了。	(作定语 attributive)

复谓结构大致分为三种:连谓结构(连动式),递系结构(兼语式),连锁结构(紧缩式)。

Double predicative structures fall into three main types: linked predicative structures (related verbs), ranked structure (concurrency), chain structure (tightly connected).

第二节　连谓结构
Linked Predicative Structure

特点：两个谓词性成分说明同一个主语。

两个谓词性成分之间的意义有如下几种：

Features: Two predicative units relate to the same subject. The semantic relationships between the two predicative units may be of the following types:

打电话通知他　　坐飞机去

（方式 way）

等一会儿再来　　吃完饭再走

（次序 order）

去医院看病人　　上街买菜

（目的 purpose）

（电视）开着没人看　　灯开着不亮

（转折 transition）

（那个人）坐着不动　　抓住不放

（同位 appositive）

看起来不好看　　走下去很危险

（假设 suppositional）

病了没上班　　没时间参加

（原因 cause）

连谓结构不同于联合结构、述宾结构和介词结构。试比较：

Linked predicative structures are not the same as compound structures, verb-object structures, or prepositional phrases. Compare the following:

他不停地抽烟喝茶。

(联合结构作谓语　compound structure as predicate)

他喜欢(一个人)看电视。

(述宾结构作宾语　verb object structure as object)

他疼得掉下眼泪。

(述宾结构作补语　verb object structure as complement)

他在草地上躺着。

(介宾结构作状语　preposition object structure as adverbial)

而连谓结构的第一个动作和第二个动作同时说明两个主语。例如：

The first and second action of the linked predicative structure may have two subjects. For example:

他带着孩子逛公园。

你陪着客人喝酒。

我扶着老人上车。

表示趋向的动词"来""去"既可出现在第二个谓词性成分之前，又可以出现在第二个谓词性成分之后，还可以重复出现。例如：

The verbs 来 and 去 which express direction may appear in front of the second predicative unit or after the second predicative unit, or may appear twice.

For example:

我去买菜。

（"去"的目的是"买菜" The purpose of 去 is 买菜）

我买菜去。

（"去"虚化，轻读 去 has no actual meaning read lightly）

我去$_1$ 买菜去$_2$。

（"去$_1$"是实动；"去$_2$"是虚动 去$_1$is a real action, 去$_2$ has no actual meaning）

"给"组成的连谓结构：

Linked predicative structure using "gei".

送一本书给他。

（"送"有"给予"的意义 送 means 给予）

送给他一本书。

（双宾语句 double object）

给他买一本书。

（"给"是介词；"买"无"给予"意义 给 is a preposition. 买 doesn't mean 给予）

"有"组成的连谓结构：

Linked predicative structure using 有：

有可能下雨。（有下雨的可能 possibility）

有钱买房子。（有买房子的钱 possession）

有话慢慢说。（表示假设 supposition）

有事出去了。（表示原因 cause）

有一米七高。（表示长度 length）

有半年没回家。（表示时间 time）

第三节 递系结构
Ranked Structure

一、递系结构里的第一个动词是有限制的

The first verb in a ranked structure is restricted.

1. 第一个动词是表示使令意义的,如"请、让、叫、使、命令"等。

The first verb expresses the idea of a command, e. g. 请,让,叫,使,命令,etc.

请你帮我买张票。
叫他们去请医生。
让他明天再来。
使大家感到奇怪。
通知他去开会。
命令大家休息。
派人去支援灾区。

2. 第一个动词是表示心理状态的动词,如"爱、恨、喜欢、怪、嫌、埋怨、感谢"等。

The first verb expresses mental state or attitude, e. g. 爱,恨,喜欢,怪,嫌,埋怨,感谢,etc.

喜欢他能干。
怪他多管闲事。

恨他不关心人。

嫌他多事。

埋怨他不按时来。

感谢大家给我的支持。

3．第一个动词是“有”、“没有”或“是”。

The first verb is 有 or 没有.

有人不信。

有颗星星落下来了。

没人知道。

有个运动员叫李宁。

是他救了那个小孩。

二、第一个述语的宾语跟后一个述语有某种意义上的联系

The object of the first verb has a certain semantic relationship with the following verb.

1．宾语是后面谓词性成分的施事。

The object is the agent of the following predicative unit.

请他来。

通知他去开会。

选他当代表。

感谢你帮助了我。

埋怨他来晚了。

2．宾语是后面谓词性成分的受事。

The object is the patient of the following predicative unit.

借本书看。

倒杯水喝。

买个西瓜吃。

3. 前一个宾语是施事,后一个宾语是受事。

The first object is the agent; the second object is the patient.

给我本书看。

借我自行车骑一下。

4. 前一个宾语是受事,后一个宾语是施事。

The first object is the patient; the second object is the agent.

买点花生大家吃。

借架相机我用。

5. 后面的谓词性成分说明前面宾语的性质。

The second predicative unit describes the character of the preceding object.

嫌他年纪轻。

称赞他勇敢。

6. 第一个动词是"有、是、在"等。

The first verb is 有,是,在,etc.

有人掉水里了。

没人知道。

是他救了那个小孩。

在他看来。

递系结构跟主谓结构作宾语的动宾结构的不同:

Ranked structures are different from verb-object structures in which subject-predicate constructions serve as objects.

1. 停顿不同。递系结构停顿的位置在第一个宾语后,主谓结构作宾语的动宾结构停顿在第一个动词后。

Pauses are different. The pause in a ranked structure comes after the first object. The pause in a verb-object structure in which a subject-predicate construction serves as object comes after the first verb.

你通知他‖来开会。　　（递系结构）

我知道‖他走了。　　（主谓结构作宾语）

2. 递系结构的第一个动词和宾语之间不能插入其他成分，主谓结构作宾语的动宾结构的第一个动词和宾语之间可以插入其他成分。

No other elements may be inserted between the first verb and its object in a ranked structure; in the verb-object structure in which a subject-predicate construction serves as object, other elements may be inserted between the first verb and its object. For example:

*我喜欢以后他能干。　（递系结构）

我希望以后你常来。　（主谓结构作宾语）

第四节　连锁结构
Chain Structure

特点：各部分靠一定的虚词连接起来。

Features: Each part is dependent on a function word for connection.

一看就明白。（时间 time）

非去不可。（逻辑 logic）

不看不知道。（条件 condition）

越学越聪明。(程度 degree)

边走边谈。(同时进行 two actions simultaneously)

上面的虚词都是前后呼应的。下面只有一个虚词连接:

The function words above echoes each other; those below have only one function word for connection. For example:

不懂就问。

有时间就去。

天黑了才走。

下课再谈。

要走就走。

死也不放。

连锁结构又叫紧缩句。它和复句的区别主要看两个动词之间有没有停顿。如果有停顿就是复句,没有停顿就是紧缩句。所谓紧缩只是两个主谓结构之间的紧缩,语义重心在后一个主谓结构上。例如:

The chain structure can also be called a tightly connected phrase.

To distinguish a chain structure from a complex sentence the important thing to consider is whether or not there is a pause between the two verbs. If there is a pause, then it is a complex sentence; if not, it is a tightly connected phrase. The so-called tightly connected phrase implies the tight connection between the two subject-predicate constructions. The semantic heart is in the second subject-predicate construction. For example:

不信你到我家里看看。

怎么说他也不听。

孩子大了管不了了。

打死我也不告诉你。

你想去你就去。

我吃过饭就去找你。

答应了就一定要办。

连锁结构和连谓结构的区别:

Differences between the chain structure and the linked predicative structure:

1. 看副词表示的是不是副词所具有的意义。如果是副词所具有的意义,就不是连锁结构,而是连谓结构;如果不是副词具有的意义,就是连锁结构。

If what the adverb is expressing is its true meaning, then it is not a chain structure but a linked predicative structure. If it is not the true meaning of the adverb, then it is a chain structure.

<table>
<tr><td>你问他就知道了。
(“就”表示关联 showing interrelation)
他想说又说不出来。
(“又”起关联作用 connecting)</td><td>连锁结构
chain structure</td></tr>
<tr><td>他上课就打瞌睡。
(“就”表示强调 emphasis)
他拿回家又看了看。
(“又”表示重复 repetition)</td><td>连谓结构
linked predicative structure</td></tr>
</table>

2. 副词起修饰作用时要重读,起关联作用时要轻读。

Adverbs used as qualifiers should be emphasized; those used as connection should be spoken lightly.

3. 关联的作用是前后两方面,修饰的作用只在后边。

The connecting function is for both parts while the qualifying function applies only to the second part.

练　　习

一、指出下列各句哪些是连谓结构，哪些是递系结构，哪些是连锁结构：

1．我给朋友写信。

2．这种水果吃起来很香。

3．车到山前必有路。

4．不当家不知柴米贵。

5．有话尽管说，不要客气。

6．他有理由不去。

7．他们上个星期去亚运村劳动了。

8．你去弄点水来。

9．学校派他出国学习。

10．没有个性，不成其为作家。

11．他在阳台上给花浇水呢。

12．拿着工资不干事。

13．恨铁不成钢。

14．越是民族的东西，越是能走向世界。

15．没有继承，就没有发展。

16．小心没错。

二、把下列各句改为连动句：

1．他买了一辆摩托车，花了一千多元。

2．他不回答我的问题，是没有理由的。

3．住那么好的房子，我现在还没有条件。

4．他上个月去了趟欧洲，是作为考察团的成员去的。

5. 他没回过家,有四年多了。

6. 度过眼前的困难,他们还是有信心的。

7. 他出国了,病刚好没多久。

8. 他会得到冠军,也许有希望。

9. 这种天气穿皮大衣,实在没必要。

二、举例说明递系结构与主谓结构作宾语的动词结构的不同。

三、用层次分析法分析下列句法结构:

1. 听老红军讲故事

2. 请老红军讲故事

3. 选他当厂长

4. 同意他当厂长

5. 你去叫他快点把书送来

第五章 复 句
Chapter Five The Double-Clause Sentence

第一节 什么是复句?
What Is a Double-Clause Sentence?

前面我们在介绍句子的类型时,曾经介绍过句子可分为单句和复句。单句又分为主谓句和非主谓句。主谓句是由主谓结构组成的句子,非主谓句是由主谓结构以外的结构组成的句子。

When we introduce the various types of sentences above, we said that sentences are divided into simple sentences and double-clause sentences. Simple sentences are further divided into subject-predicate sentences and non-subject-predicate sentences. Subject-predicate sentence is composed of a subject and a predicate while the non-subject-predicate sentence is one formed with structures other than a subject predicate structure.

复句是由两个或两个以上的分句按一定语法关系组成的句子。例如:

Double-clause sentences consist of two or more clauses which are formed into a sentence based on specific grammatical relationships. For example:

你们吃什么,我也吃什么。

时间就是生命,时间就是速度。

大家都很累,可是都很愉快。

他不但是一个爱国诗人,而且是一个爱人民的诗人。

我想送他一件礼物,可是不知道送什么好。

他虽然去过那个地方,但是记不清了。

第二节　复句的特点
Characteristics of Double-Clause Sentences

1. 复句至少有两个分句组成,各分句之间在意义上有联系。

A double-clause sentence has at least two clauses which are related in meaning.

他学中文,我也学中文。

小王刚走,你就来了。

2. 复句中,分句与分句之间停顿较短,书面上用逗号或分号隔开。而单句与单句之间停顿较长,书面上用句号隔开。

In a double-clause sentence, the pause between clauses is relatively short and, in writing, the clauses are separated by a comma or semicolon. The pause between two simple sentences is longer and they are separated by a period.

3．复句中的两个分句是平行的，彼此没有包含关系。

The two clauses are equal in status and there is no embedding.

夺取全国胜利，这只是万里长征走完了第一步。

那些没有价值的书，他从来不看。

这古老的都城，在黑夜里，依然露出她的美丽。

他藏在他看得见我，我看不见他的地方。

你去，我也去。

显然，前面的四个句子都是单句，尽管句子较长，但彼此有包含关系。第五个句子虽然短，却是两个平行的分句，彼此没有包含关系，所以是复句。

The first four sentences are simple sentences in spite of their long patterns, because there is embedding. Whereas, though the fifth sentence is short, it has two equal clauses and there is no embedding so it is a double-clause sentence.

4．复句里，分句之间的意义关系一般用连词或有关联作用的副词来表示。

The semantic relationships between the clauses of a double-clause sentence is expressed with a conjunction or conjunctive adverb.

因为下雨，所以我没去。

这种花很好看，可是却不香。

要是没时间，你就别来了。

他又爱看电影，又爱滑冰。

由以上特点看，“复句是由单句构成的”这句话很不严格。复句不是两个单句的组合，复句里的分句不是独立完整的句子；分句和分句之间的关系也不是词组和词组之间的关系。

We can see from the above characteristics that, “Double-clause sentences are constructed from simple sentence"is not a very strict statement. A double-clause sentence is not the combination of two simple sentences. The clauses in a double clause sentence are not complete, independent sentences and the relationships between the clauses is not the relationship of one phrase to another.

第三节　复句的分类
Different Types of Double-Clause Sentences

按照复句中分句之间的语法关系可以将复句分为联合复句和偏正复句两大类。

Based on grammatical relationships between the clauses, double-clause sentences can be divided into two major types: compound and endocentric.

一、联合复句　Compound sentences

联合复句包括并列、连贯、对比、选择、分合和递进等复句关系。

Compound sentences include such clause relationships as parallel, consistancy, comparison, choice, separation-combination, and ranking.

1. 并列复句:两个分句之间关系平等,没有主次之分。

Parallel sentences: The two clauses are equal in relationship, without the difference of being primary or secondary.

客人进了屋,他一面让座,一面倒茶。

河水很深,水流又急。

书市上摆满了各种书,既有中文的,又有外文的。

今年夏天,他大学毕业了,同时考上了出国研究生。

那个人又能抽烟,又能喝酒。

密云县有个大水库,水库边上有棵大槐树,大槐树下有个李老五,李老五是个万元户。

2. 连贯复句:两个分句在时间上连贯。

Consistancy sentences: The two clauses are consistant in time.

他前脚刚走,小张后脚进了屋。

他去邮局发了封信,又到书店买了本书。

他把晾干的衣服收回来,叠整齐,放在柜子里。

商店刚开门,就进来好些人。

人齐了,会就开始了。

3. 对比复句:两个分句是一种对比关系。

Comparison sentences: The two clauses are comparing or contrasting.

南方多云转阴,北方晴间多云。

冬天干冷,夏天湿热。

男的一律骑自行车,女的都乘公共汽车。

不是我不愿意去,而是他不让我去。

我们熟悉的东西有些快要闲起来了，我们不熟悉的东西正在强迫我们去做。

4. 选择复句：两个分句是一种选择关系。

Choice sentences: The two sentences are two choices for one to make.

不是你去，就是我去。
要么这个星期天去，要么下个星期天去。 } 二者取一
或者你来，或者我去找你。

吃烤鸭还是吃饺子？
是找人修还是自己修呢？ } (是……还是……)

与其挤车，不如骑车去。
宁可断其一指，不可伤其十指。 } (取舍)

5. 分合复句：复句呈现先合后分或先分后合的形式。

Generalizing-specializing sentences: First generalize, then specialize, or vice versa.

消灭老鼠的办法有两种：一种是养猫，一种是用药。

历史上的战争分为两类：一类是正义的，一类是非正义的。

在改革中，我们坚持两条根本原则：一是社会主义公有制经济占主体，一是共同富裕。

或者把老虎打死，或者被老虎吃掉，二者必居其一。

6. 递进复句：后一分句补充前一分句的内容。

Ranking sentences: The latter clause supplements the first clause.

他不但去过英国,而且去过意大利。

不但产量增加了,人的精神面貌也变了。

小王不但会骑摩托车,还会开汽车。

他不仅要去上海,还要去四川。

这样做不但没有解决矛盾,反而增加了矛盾。

中国是联合国的创始成员国,又是安理会的常任理事国。

二、偏正复句 Endocentric sentences

偏正复句包括转折、假设、条件、目的、因果、倚变、时间等复句关系。

Including such clause relationships as transition, supposition, condition, purpose, cause and effect, change and time.

1. 转折复句:在意义上,两个分句之间呈转折关系。

Transition sentences: Showing transition in meaning between the two clauses.

(1) 一般转折:用加强后一个分句突出后者,连词在后。

General transition: The conjunction is on the second part to show emphasis.

雨已经停了,可是风还在刮。

别人都去旅行了,然而他还在犹豫。

他和我都在北大学习,只是他比我早来一年。

我喜欢打网球,不过打得不好。

(2) 让步转折:用减弱前一个分句来突出后者,连词在前。

Concessive transition: The conjunction is on the first part to weaken the first clause and thus stress the second clause.

我虽然学了三年中文,但是听相声还有困难。

尽管天气很冷,我仍然坚持早晨跑步。

这衣服好是好,就是价钱太贵了。

虽然时间很紧张,可是过得很愉快。

(3) 假设让步转折:前提虚拟。

Suppositional concessive transition: The precondition is suppositional.

即使下大雪,我也要去。

就是再便宜,我也不买。

就算你说的对,那又怎么样?

哪怕困难再大,我们也不怕。

2. 假设复句:前一分句是后一分句的假设条件。

Suppositional sentences: The first clause is the suppositional condition of the second clause.

如果你不方便,可以换一个时间。

如果小王来了,叫他找我一下。

要是你有什么困难,就告诉我。

即使条件再好,也要靠自己努力。

即使你说错了,那也没什么关系。

学了不用,即使学得再多,也没有用。

哪怕人再多,我也敢说。

哪怕这件事与我无关,我也要管。

你再闹,我就不理你了。

3. 条件复句:后一分句以前一分句为条件。

Conditional sentences: The second clause is the precondition of the first clause.

(1) 充分条件　Full condition

只要你说的对,我们就改正。

只要下功夫,你就一定能学会。

只要你愿意,一切都好办。

(2) 唯一条件　Sole condition

只有实践,才能获得正确的答案。

只有他爱人才最了解他的脾气。

要想很快富裕起来,只有搞活经济。

除非你答应了他的要求,他才会离开的。

除非你不去,他也不去。

若要人不知,除非己莫为。

(3) 无条件(任指)　No condition (general reference)

不管困难有多大,我们也要克服。

不管来不来,你都给我来个电话。

无论天热天冷,他总是穿得很多。

无论做什么工作,他都很认真。

不论大事还是小事,大家都愿意找他商量。

不论哪门功课,他都学得很好。

4. 目的复句:一个分句以另一分句为目的。

Purpose sentences: One clause is the purpose of another.

为了加快四化建设,中国正在进行经济体制的改革。

我把电话号码告诉你,免得你来回跑了。

你应该早早做好准备,以免到时候手忙脚乱。

我事先告诉你,为的是你有个思想准备。

为了早日恢复健康,他搬到郊区农村来住。

5. 因果复句:两个分句之间存在因果关系。

Cause-effect sentence: The relation between the two clauses are cause and effect.

因为天气不好,飞机没能起飞。

由于治疗不及时,病情恶化了。

既然学过了,就没有必要再学了。

他之所以来晚了,是因为路上遇到了麻烦。

我们不能因为一件小事,而影响了同志间的关系。

6. 倚变复句:后一分句随着前一分句的变化而变化。

Complying sentences: The second clause changes according to the first clause.

你有多少,我要多少。

你去哪儿,我们也去哪儿。

你说怎么干,我们就怎么干。

你越是摆架子,群众越不买你的账。

你吃什么,我们就吃什么。

7. 时间复句(表示时间的是一个句子,而不是时间词)

Time sentences: A clause but not a time word is used to indicate time.

我刚进屋,电话铃就响了。

我还没出门,就下起雨来了。

火车还没到站,站台上已经站满了人。

等我赶到现场,人已经走光了。

天一黑,路灯就亮了。

第四节　多重复句
Multi-Clause Sentence

包含两个或两个以上结构层次的复句,叫多重复句。例如:
A sentence which has three or more clauses is called a multi-clause sentence. For example:

因为我们是为人民服务的,|所以我们如果
　　　　　　　　　　　　因果
有缺点,‖就不怕别人批评指出。
　　　假设

只有像解放军英模报告团那样,既讲得好,
‖又做得好,|才能受到人们的欢迎。
并列　　　　条件

既然讲演的目的是教育群众,‖讲演者本
　　　　　　　　　　　　　因果
身就得做出个样子,|否则不但起不了传播精神
　　　　　　　　　转折
文明的作用,‖ 反而会给人们留下不好的影响。
　　　　　　递进

即使有了汽车、摩托、彩电、冰箱,‖ 乃至现
　　　　　　　　　　　　　　　递进
代化管理制度,|如果使用这些设备和实行这种
　　　　　　　假设
制度的人自身还未从精神上和观念上经历现代
化的转变,‖那么,现代化的变革出现畸型的发
　　　　　假设
展甚至失败的结局都有可能。

在自然科学发展的历史中,有不少科学家

认识了真理，‖并且坚持了真理，|结果被反动
　　　　　　递进　　　　　　因果

的统治者杀死、烧死，‖他们的著作也被禁止烧
　　　　　　　　　递进

毁。

分析多重复句，要注意弄清分句之间的意义上的联系，还要弄清各复句之间的层次关系，还要弄清关联词语之间的交叉情况。

In analyzing the multi-clause sentence it is important to clarify the semantic relationships between clauses, to clarify the levels of relationship of the clauses, and to understand the ways in which the conjunctive words are related.

练　　习

一、指出下列句子哪些是单句，哪些是复句：

1. 他主张不能只关心自己的家事，还要关心国家和全世界的大事。

2. 唐代的诗最多最好，宋代的词最多最好，所以文学史上有"唐诗"和"宋词"的名称。

3. 这是一种既复杂却又单纯，既悲伤却又欢喜，既无奈却又无怨的心情。

4. 友谊和花香一样，还是淡一点的比较好，越淡的香气越使人依恋，也越能长久。

5. 取得亚洲冠军，不过是走向世界的第一步。

6. 你不要以为自己最聪明，别人都是傻瓜。

7. 人只有献身于社会，才能找出那短暂而有风险的生命的意

义。

8．任何一种对时间的点滴浪费，都无异于一种慢性的自杀。

9．他是想来就来，不想来就不来的自由惯了的一种人。

10．摄影不仅是一只科学的眼睛，也是一只艺术的眼睛、神奇的眼睛。

二、分析下列复句，并说明各分句之间的关系：

1．他的声音不大，但是很有力。（　　）

2．既然大夫说能治好，你就不要再担心了。（　　）

3．我们熟悉的东西有些快要闲起来了，我们不熟悉的东西正在强迫我们去做。（　　）

4．尽管我看过这部电影，我还想再看一次。（　　）

5．即使你看过了，也可以再看看。（　　）

6．除非他向我承认错误，否则我是不会答应的。（　　）

7．无论条件怎样艰苦，他都不怕。（　　）

三、指出下列复句的类型：

1．如果事情都像你想的那样简单，就好了。

2．他把手里的工作交给了小王，就匆匆走了。

3．你说的那种情况不是听来的，就是编造的。

4．尽管他说要来，我还是有点不信。

5．天还没亮，他就起床了。

6．除非是亲朋好友，他不轻易拿给别人看。

7．你说要什么，我们就给你什么。

8．我是说过要去，可我哪有时间呢？

9．他不但不听劝告，反而更凶了。

10．与其呆在家里没事，不如出去走走。

11．人有悲欢离合，月有阴晴圆缺。

12．要是你不介意，我想打开窗户。

13．只要你同意，我马上去通知他。

14. 既然大家没意见,这件事就定了。

15. 你走你的阳关道,我走我的独木桥。

16. 为了早日完成三峡工程,大家奋力苦战。

17. 无论谁去求他,他都乐意帮忙。

18. 即使找不到合适的人,也不要着急。

四、在下列各句的横线上填上适当的关联词:

1. 他________善于发现问题,________善于解决问题。
2. 这样的事情________一件两件,________很多。
3. 作家________想写出好的作品,________必须深入生活。
4. ________谎言重复一千次,________绝不会变成事实。
5. ________你不想去,那________没什么关系。
6. ________什么人去请他,他________不来。
7. ________你们早已认识,________用不着我再介绍了。
8. ________在中国,________在别的国家,______有这种花。
9. 北京的冬天,________很冷,________时间不长。
10. 大家走着去,________坐车去快一些。

五、改正下列病句:

1. 只有你坚持下去,一定能学好中文。
2. 因为他到中国的时间不长,所以已经走了不少地方。
3. 即使中国话还说不好,你就应该多练习。
4. 如果学过的生词,他都认真地记下来。
5. 哪怕下大雨,我还要去。
6. 只要我们努力,我们才学得会。
7. 我爱我们的学校,但是更爱我们的祖国。
8. 尽管什么原因,这样做都是不对的。
9. 既然他没找到,他也要想办法找到。
10. 不管天气太冷,我哪儿也没去。

六、分析下列多重复句：

1. 记忆,无论是美好的还是痛苦的,都同样珍贵,因为它属于我自己。

2. 如果对本民族的传统文化采取虚无主义的态度,就失去了吸收和消化外来文化的基础,也就根本谈不上新文化的建设和发展。

3. 全世界出现了地区性缺水现象。虽然水的不足目前在地理上还限于一些地区,但是如果继续无节制地用水,这种状况肯定会扩大。

4. 我们不论认识什么事物,都必须全面地去看,不但要看到它的正面,也要看到它的反面,否则,就不能有比较完全和正确的认识。

5. 保持健康的唯一办法是:吃你所不愿吃的东西,喝你所不爱喝的饮料,做你所不想做的事情。

6. 我们的工资一般还不高,但是因为就业的人多了,因为物价低而稳,加上其他种种条件,工人的生活比过去还是有了很大改善。

第六章　虚　　词
Chapter Six　Function Words

虚词是对实词而言的。虚词不表示实在的意义,它只表示抽象的语法意义。虚词不能单用,不能充当句子成分。汉语中的虚词大约有七百多个,数量远比实词要少得多,但在语法中占有十分重要的地位。下面只介绍其中最常用的几个。

Function words contrast with notional words. Function words do not express an actual notional meaning but simply express an abstract grammatical meaning. Function words cannot be used alone or fill any of the slots for sentence elements. There are about 700 function words in Chinese, not nearly so many as there are notional words, but in terms of grammar they play a very important role. Below we will introduce only the most frequently used ones.

第一节　把

一、"把"的意义　The meaning of 把

"把"是介词,它的意义在于表示处置。

把 is a preposition. The meaning of 把 is related to management or disposal. For example:

把花盆放在阳台上。

把教室打扫得干干净净。

"花盆""教室"是处置的对象,"把"的作用在于强调后面动作的主动性。

花盆 is the object to be disposed. The function of 把 is to stress the activeness of the following action.

传统语法学家认为"把"字句是从常式句"主—谓—宾"式变来的,"把"字的作用在于把宾语提前。例如:

Traditional grammarians believed that the 把 construction was a rearrangement of the commonly used "subject-verb-object" form. 把 was used to prepose the object. For example:

把信发了	←发了信
把屋子收拾收拾	←收拾收拾屋子
把钢笔还你	←还你钢笔
把窗户关上	←关上窗户
把问题搞清楚	←搞清楚问题

"把"字句是不是从"主—谓—宾"式变来的呢?"把"字的作用是不是把宾语提到动词前边来呢?那就要看宾语是否能还原回去。从实际情况看,大部分的"把"字句都不能还原为"主—谓—宾"式。例如:

Is the 把 construction a transformation of the "S-V-O" form? Is it used to put the object before the verb? It is necessary to see if the object can be returned to the original position. In fact, most 把 constructions cannot be rearranged as "S-V-O." For example:

把画挂在墙上	*挂画在墙上
把东西放在桌上	*放东西在桌上

把石头变成金子　　　　*变石头成金子

把客人接到家里　　　　*接客人到家里

把小说改编成电影　　　*改编小说成电影

既然这些句子不能还原回去,就无所谓是从常式句变来的,也就谈不上宾语提前,因为这个宾语原本就可以出现在动词前面。

Since these sentences cannot be rearranged, it can't be considered as a transformation of S-V-O, nor the preposing of the object.

二、"把"字句的特点和用法 Characteristics and the usage of 把:

1. "把"字句中的动词是有限的,必须是及物动词。

Verbs which may be used with 把 are restrained. The verbs in a 把 construction must be transitive.

发(信)　关(门)　还(钢笔)　收拾(屋子)

及物动词中有些不能用于"把"字句。大致有以下几类:

Not all transitive verbs can be used with 把. Following are some which may not be used:

(1) 表示趋向的动词　Directional verb:进、出、上、下、走、进去、进来、出去、出来、离开。

(2) 表示心理活动的动词　Verbs showing mental activities: 觉得、以为、希望、同情、信、赞成。

(3) "是、有、在、到、像、属于、成为"一类动词。

(4) "看见、听见、碰见、遇到、得到、接近"等表示意外的动词。Verbs showing accidental actions.

以上归纳的几类也有例外的情况。例如:

There are exceptions for the above four types.

我把他恨死了。

(“恨”是表示心理活动的动词)

(恨 is a verb showing mental activity)

我把手表丢了。

(“丢”是表示意外的动词)

(丢 is a verb showing accidental action)

2. “把”字句中,动词必须是复杂形式。动词不能是单个动词,前后总要有其他成分。

The verbs used in 把 constructions cannot be simple verbs but must be complex with additional elements.

For example:

把门锁上	(结果补语)	*把门锁
把衣服洗了	(了)	*把衣服洗
把窗户开着	(着)	*把窗户开
把屋子收拾收拾	(重叠)	*把屋子收拾
把书看完了	(结果)	*把书看
把礼物送给朋友	(动宾)	*把礼物送

3. 由“在、到、成、给”作补语的句子常用“把”字。

Sentences which have 在,到,成,给 as complements often use the 把 construction.

把箱子放在哪儿?

把客人带到客厅里。

把他看成自己人。

把信交给邮递员。

4. “把”字后面的宾语是有定的,不能省去。

The object following 把 is definite, and can't be omitted.

他把信写好了。

你把箱子打开。

我把自行车借给人了。

你把情况介绍一下。

5. 宾语是后边动词的受事(少数例外)。

The object is the patient of the verb which follows (a few exceptions)

把报纸借给我。

把牛奶取了。

把飞机票退了。

有些宾语不是动词的受事,而是整个动词结构的受事。例如:

Some objects are not the patient of the verb, but rather the patient of entire verb construction. For example:

把笔写秃了	* 写笔	写秃了笔
把脚走肿了	* 走脚	走肿了脚
把肚子笑疼了	* 笑肚子	笑疼了肚子

无论是受事还是非受事,我们都可以把"把"字句看作是:把+受事主语句。例如:

Whether patient or non-patient, we can look upon the 把 construction as 把+patient subject sentence.

把牛奶喝了。	——把+牛奶喝了
把机票退了。	——把+机票退了
把车骑走了。	——把+车骑走了
把箱子放在哪儿?	——把+箱子放在哪儿?
把钱留着。	——把+钱留着

"把"在这里强调动作的主动性。

Here 把 is used to stress the activeness of the action.

6. 助动词、否定副词必须放在“把”字前面。

Auxiliaries and negative adverbs must be placed before 把.

要把字写清楚。

应该把这个消息告诉大家。

没把杯子打破。

别把衣服弄脏了。

第二节　被

汉语里的“被”字是从动词(“覆盖”义)虚化来的,现在只作介词用。

被 in Chinese was funtionalized from the meaning of 覆盖 and is now used as a preposition.

一、“被”字句的意义和用法　The meaning and usage of 被 construction

1. 介词“被”在句子中的意义表示遭受,作用表示被动。

The preposition 被 expresses the meaning of being subjected to something. Its function is to show passiveness. For example:

甲组	乙组
树(被)刮倒了	树被风刮倒了
杯子(被)打破了	杯子被他打破了
书(被)借走了	书被别人借走了

狗(被)打死了　　　　狗被人打死了

他(被)解雇了　　　　他被老板解雇了

甲乙两组的主语都是后边动词的受事。因而,被字句事实上也是受事主语句,我们可以将甲组中的"被"字省去,这样就变成了受事主语句,"被"字在这里表示被动的意义。乙组"被"字后边的宾语是其后边动词的施事,"被"字的作用在于把施事者介绍出来,增强了动作的被动性。

The subjects in both groups are all patients of the verbs which follow. Therefore the 被 sentence is actually a sentence with a patient subject. The 被 in the first group can be omitted, making these sentences patient subject sentences. The 被 here shows passiveness. In the second group, the object which follows the 被 is the agent of the following verb. So the function of 被 is still to introduce the agent and emphasize the passive nature of the action.

2. "被"后面的宾语可以省去。有些宾语不出现是由于说不出或不必说出。

The object following 被 can be omitted. Some objects are omitted because they can't be named or it is unnecessary to name them. For example:

书被借走了。　(宾语省去 object omitted)

书被(别人)借走了。

(不必具体说出 unnecessary to tell)

狗被(人)打死了。(说不出 unable to tell)

这样做会被(人)看不起。

("人"指任何人 indicates anyone)

3. 被字句表示的事情对于受事者来说常常是不如意或不企望的。

The matter expressed in a 被 sentence is undesirable or unexpected for the patient. For example:

他被抓起来了。

他被公司解雇了。

眼镜不小心被打碎了。

刚买的新衣服就被你弄脏了。

但有些被字句并不表示不如意或不企望的。

But there are exceptions.

他被人救了。

他被大家选为代表。

4. 有些"被"字句里的动词后边另有宾语。

Verbs in certain 被 sentences are followed by an additional object. For example:

他被人打断了一条腿。

（宾语从属主语　The object is related to subject）

他的事迹被写成小说。

（宾语是动作的结果　The object is the result of the verb）

他被人打了一棍子。

（宾语是工具　The object is a tool）

他被人告到法院。

（宾语是处所　The object is the place）

5. 否定词放在"被"字之前。

The negative word must be placed before 被 .

这种情况一直不被人重视。

幸亏没被人看见。

6. "被"和"所"组成"被……所……"式。

The forming of 被…所… pattern.

被生活所迫。

被他的话所感动。

被坏人所利用。

被环境所支配。

表示被动意义的介词除了"被"字以外,还有"让""叫""给",但用法上略有不同。

In addition to 被,other prepositions which express the passive meaning are 让,叫,给. There are slight differences in usage.

1. "让""叫"后边一般要带宾语,"被""给"不一定。

让 and 叫 are usually followed by an object; 被 and 给 may sometimes not. For example:

你们俩的秘密让小王听见了。

鱼叫猫吃了。

她给(蛇)吓了一跳。

2. "被""让""叫"之后主要动词之前可以加"给"。

The main verb following 被,让,and 叫 can be preceded by 给. For example:

杯子被他给打破了。

这孩子的病叫大夫给耽误了。

她让父母给惯坏了。

"被"字句表示被动意义,但表示被动意义的句子不一定用"被"字。例如:

The 被 sentence expresses the passive meaning, but passive sentences do not necessarily have to use 被. For example:

眼镜是我打破的。

自行车小王骑走了。

二、“把”字句和“被”字句的区别 Differences between 把 sentences and 被 sentences

从语义上看，“把”字的宾语是后面动词的受事，“被”字的宾语是后面动词的施事；“把”字的作用在于表示处置，“被”字的作用在于表示被动。

从结构上看，“把”字的宾语必须出现，“被”字的宾语可以不出现；“把”字句中动词前后必须有其他成分，“被”字句中动词前后不一定出现其他成分。

In terms of semantics, the object of 把 is the patient of the verb which follows; the object of 被 is the agent of the verb which follows. The function of 把 is to express management; the function of 被 is to express passiveness.

From the standpoint of structure, the object of 把 must be expressed, but the object of 被 can be left unexpressed. In the 把 sentence, the verb must be preceded and followed by other elements; while in the 被 sentence, the verb may or may not have other elements.

练　习

一、把下列句子改为“把”字句：

1. 他在楼前停车。
2. 他布置房间很雅致。
3. 你不要弄脏了书。

4. 请你介绍一下你们学校的情况。

5. 这个问题今天要讨论完。

6. 王府井他都跑遍了,也没找到合适的鞋。

二、改正下列句子中的错误:

1. 他把电影没看完就走了。

2. 他把中文学得很好。

3. 昨天在街上我把朋友遇见了。

4. 等我把钱有了就给你办婚事。

5. 我把鲁迅的小说读过了。

6. 我终于把他的话相信了。

7. 我把那个人讨厌极了。

8. 你怎么能把大家的东西属于自己呢?

三、改正下列病句:

1. 我的钱包被丢了。

2. 这种东西从来被人不注意。

3. 他被大家等了许久。

4. 电影被我看完了。

5. 鸡被养大了。

6. 他被我恨死了。

四、把"把"字句改成"被"字句:

1. 他把机票退了。

2. 你把信发了。

3. 你把人放了。

4. 他把表丢了。

5. 我把学费交了。

6. 他把命送了。

7. 我把事给忘了。

8. 谁把灯关了?

9．我把消息搞错了。

10．他把黑夜当白天。

11．他把方便让给人。

12．他把理论和实际结合起来。

13．他把温暖送给别人。

14．他把事情闹大了。

15．我把他介绍给你。

16．他把打字机弄坏了。

17．我把花浇死了。

五、用下列格式造句：

1．把……当成

2．把……变成

3．把……看成

4．把……做成

5．把……写成

6．把……画成

7．把……读成

8．把……翻译成

9．把……剃成

10．把……修成

11．把……改成

12．把……切成

13．把……分成

14．把……怕成

15．把……撕成

16．把……建设成

17．把……改造成

18．把……理解成

19. 把……折合成
20. 把……兑换成
21. 把……布置成
22. 把……打扮成
23. 把……描写成

第三节　对、对于、关于

一、对、对于

介词"对""对于"的作用是把跟谓语有关系的人和事物介绍出来。由"对""对于"组成的介词结构在句中经常作状语。

The function of the prepositions 对 and 对于 is to introduce persons or things which are related to the predicate. Prepositional structures formed with 对 and 对于 usually serve as adverbials.

他对人很热情。

我对这里的环境还不熟悉。

对于他的进步,我们都感到高兴。

你的意见对于改进我们的工作很有帮助。

可是,"对"和"对于"的用法不都相同。一般说来,能用"对于"的地方,也能用"对"。可是,能用"对"的地方不一定都能用"对于"。

But the usage of 对 and 对于 are not entirely the same. Generally speaking, places where 对于 can be used, 对 can also be used; but when 对 can be used; it is not always possible to use 对于.

对于经济方面的理论学得太少。

对于过去的事情就不要再提了。

对于学习上有困难的同学要多帮助。

你对我说的话我没有忘记。

这个人你对他了解吗?

上面例句中,前三句中的“对于”都可以换成“对”,后两句中的“对”不能换成“对于”。这是因为“对”的动作性很强,由“对”组成的介词结构后面不能有停顿。

“对于”后面的宾语有时在意义上是后面动词的受事。

In the examples above,对于 could be replaced by 对 in the first three sentences. In the last two sentence,对 cannot be replaced by 对于. This is because of the dynamic nature of 对;there cannot be a pause after prepositional structures using 对.

Sometimes the object following 对于 is the semantic patient of the verb which follows.

对于新的交通规则我还不十分了解。

对于我们工作中的问题,必须认真解决。

“交通规则”在意义上是“了解”的受事,“问题”在意义上是“解决”的受事。

In terms of semantics 交通规则 is the patient of 了解,and 问题 is the patient of 解决.

二、对于、关于

“对于”主要是指出对象,“关于”主要是表示关涉。凡是对象确定的,只用“对于”不能用“关于”。

对于 usually points out an object or target;关于 expresses the

idea of in relation to something. Whenever a target is definite only 对于 can be used;关于 is not appropriate.

对于未来的前途,我们充满了信心。

吸烟对于人的健康不利。

对于过去的历史人物,我们都应采取历史唯物主义的态度。

对于涉及群众利益的问题,应该公开。

"关于"是指出范围或提示性质,一般用于句首。

When 关于 points out range or boundary or shows characteristics, it usually comes at the beginning of the sentence.

关于今后的任务,要提前安排。

关于联大会议,你有什么看法?

"关于"组成的介词结构有时可以作定语。

Sometimes the prepositional structures formed with 关于 can be attributives. For example:

他买了一本关于二次大战的历史书。

关于公费医疗改革的讨论仍在进行。

第四节　在、给、比

一、在

由介词"在"组成的介词结构可以放在动词前,也可以放在动词后。

Prepositional structure using 在 can be placed either before or after the verb.

在学校住

住在学校

但是,由"在"组成的介词结构并不是可以放在任何动词的前面或后面,有的只能放在前面,有的只能放在后面,有的既可以放在前面又可以放在后面。

But prepositional structures formed with 在 cannot be placed before or after every verb. Some can be placed only in front, others only after, still others can be used in either place.

只能放在动词前面的 Those which must precede the verb:

在湖里游泳　　*游泳在湖里

在屋里看书　　*看书在屋里

在餐厅吃饭　　*吃饭在餐厅

在楼前等车　　*等车在楼前

只能放在动词后面的 Those which must follow the verb:

手表掉在海里　　*在海里掉手表

信投在邮筒里　　*在邮筒里投信

话说在点子上　　*在点子上说话

雨点打在窗户上　　*在窗户上打雨点

既能放在动词前又能放在动词后的 Those which can be placed before or after the verb:

在床上躺着　　躺在床上

在院子里站着　　站在院子里

在墙上挂照片　　照片挂在墙上

在池子里养鱼　　鱼养在池子里

可见,由"在"组成的介词结构出现在什么位置上是有条件的。

当表示动作发生的处所是动态的，由“在”组成的介词结构只能出现在动词前。当表示动作的趋向是动态的，它只能出现在动词之后。当表示人或事物所处的位置是静态的，它既能出现在动词前又能出现在动词后。

值得注意的是，“在山上盖房子”既可以理解动作发生的处所是动态的，即人在山上盖房子，又可以理解为事物所处的位置是静态的，即房子盖在山上。

There are certain conditions which determine where prepositional structures using 在 will be placed. When the location of the action is dynamic, the prepositional structures may appear only before the verb. When the direction of the action is dynamic, it can appear only after the verb. When a stative situation is expressed, the prepositional structure may appear before or after the verb.

It is worth noting that a phrase such as 在山上盖房子 can be understood in the dynamic sense “Someone is building a house on the mountain”, or it can be understood in the stative sense “The house is built on the mountain.”

二、给

介词“给”的用法有两种：

There are two ways to use the preposition 给.

1. 和“被”相同，用在受事主语句里，引出施事者。

Same as 被, when used with a patient subject, it points out agent.

他给人骗了。

鱼给猫吃了。

衣服给雨淋湿了。

大火给军民扑灭了。

"给"有时也能同"被、让、叫、把"等介词用在一起。

给 can sometimes be used with the prepositions 被,让,叫,and 把.

话被小王给听见了。

你让他给蒙在鼓里。

孩子叫狼给叼走了。

你把事情给弄颠倒了。

这里的"给"也可以不出现。

This 给 can be omitted.

2. 引出受益或受损的与事来。

It points out the source of gain or loss.

坏人给抓住了。

电话给我接通了。

他给气出病来了。

手给刺扎出血来了。

三、比

介词"比"用来表示比较事物的性状或动作行为的程度。其格式是"甲 + 比 + 乙 + 谓"。

The preposition 比 is used to express comparison in the condition of things or the degree of action or behavior. The pattern is A + 比 + B + predicate.

他比我忙。

这座城市比那座城市漂亮。

今天比昨天冷。

他比我了解情况。

我比他喜欢运动。

他比我学习好。

1．谓语如果是形容词，前后可带表示数量或程度的成分。

If the predicate is an adjective, it can be preceded or followed by numeral measure words or degree words.

他比我小两岁。

这间屋子比那间屋子大得多。

北京冬天气温比上海低七八度。

2．谓语动词限于表示能力、愿望、爱好或增减的动词。

Verbs used in these predicates must show ability, will, likes, or gain or loss.

他比我会下棋。

他比我想上学。

他比别人喜欢滑冰。

车祸比去年同期上升百分之五。

3．谓语是一般行为动词，动词带“得”后，“比”的位置可以在动词前，也可以在动词后。

If the predicate is an ordinary verb of behavior followed by 得，比 may come either before or after the verb.

他比我走得快。　　——他走得比我快。

他比我写得好。　　——他写得比我好。

他比我来得早。　　——他来得比我早。

4．相同事物的比较限于时间词。

A comparison between the same things must use time words.

他比过去胖了。

今年的收成比往年要好。

"比"前后时间重复表示程度累进。

To express degree, use repetition of time words.

天气一天比一天冷。

收入一年比一年多。

要求一次比一次高。

5. 否定词一般放在"比"前。

Negatives usually precede 比.

他不比我年轻。

他来得不比我早。

第五节　再、又

一、再

"再"是时间副词,表示程度、范围。

再 is a time adverb which expresses degree and range.

1. 表示动作的重复或继续。

Expresses repetition or continuation of an action.

时间还早,再坐一会儿。

你再说一遍。

2. 表示一件事在另一件事之后发生。

Indicates one thing happening after another.

你吃了饭再走。

你先和他商量一下再说。

3. 表示程度高。

Expresses a high degree.

再危险我也不怕。

这样再好(也)不过了。

没有比友谊再珍贵的了。

4. 表示让步假设。

Hypothetical concession.

你说得再好,他也不信。

即使再冷,也不会很冷了。

你的钱再多,那又有什么用呢?

5. 表示永远消失,不复存在。(起加强语气的作用)

Indicates permanent extinction, never to occur or appear again (used for emphasis).

我再也不信他那一套了。

他再也不会回来了。

我再也忍不住了。

二、又

"又"的用法有三种:

又 has three usages:

1. 表示一个动作重复发生,或两个动作相继发生。

Expresses the reoccurrence of an action or two successive actions.

他找了一遍又一遍,还是没找到。

他昨天来过,今天又来了。

他给了我一张电影票,你又给了我一张。

明天又是星期天了。

又刮风了。

2. 表示补充。

Expresses complement.

天冷,又有风。

他聪明,又用功。

东西好,价钱又便宜。

他做错了事,又不承认。

3. 表示反复、强调等语气。

Expresses a tone of repetition or emphasis.

他又想看又不想看。
他想说又不好意思开口。 } (反复)

你别管了,又不是你的事。
他怎么会知道的? 别人又没告诉他。 } (强调)

冷又有什么关系? (反问)

第六节 不、没(有)

一、不

"不"是否定副词,不能修饰名词,只出现在动词、形容词以及其他副词或介词之前。

不 is a negative adverb; it cannot qualify nouns. It can be used only in front of verbs, adjectives, other adverbs, or prepositions.

1．出现在动词前：

In front of verbs：

不去

不看电影

不能走

2．出现在形容词前：

In front of adjectives：

不红

不坏

不干净

3．出现在副词前：

In front of adverbs：

不很好

不太感兴趣

不再讨论了

4．出现在介词前：

In front of prepositions：

不把人找回来你别想见我

不被重视

不比别人差

二、没(有)

现代汉语里有两个“没(有)”。一个是动词，如“我没(有)朋友”“那里没(有)水”；另一个是副词，如“我没(有)去”“我没(有)写信”。

There are two 没(有) in modern Chinese. One is a verb, e.g. 我没(有)朋友，那里没(有)水；the other is an adverb, e.g. 我没(有)

去,我没(有)写信.

1. 动词"没(有)"+名词性成分(否定存在的事实):

Verb 没(有)+nominal elements (negating existence):

没(有)人 ——有人

没(有)朋友 ——有朋友

没(有)工作 ——有工作

2. 副词"没(有)"+动词(否定动作、行为的发生):

Adverb 没(有)+verb (negating the happening of action or behavior):

没(有)去 ——去了

没(有)上课 ——上了

没(有)结婚 ——结婚了

3. 副词"没(有)"+形容词(否定性质、状态的变化):

Adverb 没(有)+adjective (negating changes of nature or state):

没(有)红 ——红了

没(有)坏 ——坏了

没(有)错 ——错了

第七节 都、也

一、都

"都"是表示范围的副词,它的意义是"全部"。它总括的人或事物有时在前,有时在后。

都 is an adverb expressing scope or range; it means all or

complete. The people or thing which it includes may sometimes precede and sometimes follow the word itself..

音乐、美术、体育他都喜欢。 上海、广州、西安他都想去。 先生都是中国人。 衣服都洗完了。	总括的在前 (precede 都)
你都买什么了? 屋子里都是人。	总括的在后(after 都)
跳舞我们都不会。 上海我们都去过。	总括的是"我们" (都 refers to 我们)

文学、历史和哲学我们都要学。

(总括大主语　都 refers to the major subject)

"都"的用法 Usage of 都:

1. 用于表示任指的小主语之后。

Used after the minor subject showing general reference.

他谁都不理。

他什么都会。

他哪儿都想去。

他怎么都不说。

2. 用于肯定与否定之间。

Used between positive and negative forms of a word.

树叶动都不动。

他连看都不看。

他想都不想。

3. 用于表示强调的语气。

Used to show emphasis.

长了这么大，连飞机都没坐过。

等我出来，连个人影都没看到。

他连句话都没说就走了。

4. 用于"把"字句。

Used in 把 structure.

他把攒下来的钱都捐给了灾区。

他把名字都写错了。

你可把人都得罪了。

5. 表示埋怨，说明理由。

Used to show complaint or reason.

都是你，把花给浇死了。

都是我不好，事先没有告诉大家。

6. 表示时间，相当于"已经"。

Indicating time, equivallent to 已经.

他都五十了。

现在都十二点了。

电影都开演了。

注意：表示范围的"都"要重读，表示时间的"都"要轻读。

Note: 都 which expresses scope should be stressed in reading; when expressing time it should be spoken lightly. For example:

客人ˊ都走了。 （重读·范围）

客人都走了。 （轻读·时间）

二、也

"也"表示两个事物或两种情况相同或类似。

也 expresses that two things or circumstances are similar or the same.

风停了,雨也住了。

你去,我也去。

去也可以,不去也可以。

他是人,你也是人,你怕什么?

"也"的用法 Usage of 也:

1. 疑问代词+也+不(没有、别)+动词,表示任指。

Interrogative+也+不(没有,别)+verb, showing general reference.

(这件事)谁也不知道。

(我)什么也没有买。

(你)哪儿也别去。

2. 加在重复动词之间,表示列举。

Added between two repeated verbs, showing listing.

吃也吃不好,睡也睡不好。

看也看不见,听也听不清楚。

研究也研究不出个名堂来。

3. 表示强调。

Indicating emphasis.

(1) "连……也"式:

连小学生也知道他的名字。

(强调施事 emphasize agent)

他连小说也没看过。(强调受事 emphasize patient)

我借给你的书你连看也没看。

(强调动词 emphasize verb)

(2) "再……也"式:

你再说也没有用。

猴子再聪明也还是猴子。

(3) “一……也”式:

一天假也没请过。

一次机会也不放过。

4. 表示委婉语气。

Showing a mild tone.

你也不是不明白我的意思。

他也不是想和你过不去。

话也不能这么说。

你也不小了,该知道怎么做。

5. 用在复句的第二个分句,表示条件。

Used in the second clause, showing condition.

例句		
你就是去了,也没用。	转折 transition	无条件 no condition
无论什么人,也不能特殊。		
矛盾的性质不同,解决的方法也不同。	倚变 change	
你愿意也得愿意,不愿意也得愿意。		

第八节　才、就

一、才

1. 表示动作发生的时间晚。

Expresses that the occurrence of an action is late.

你怎么现在才来?

五分钟以前,我才知道这个消息。

2．表示数量少。

Shows that a number is small.

他今年才二十岁。

一个上午他才写了几个字。

3．表示原因。

Shows cause or reason.

我看了好几遍，才看懂他的信。

大家一再追问，他才把实话说了。

4．表示强调。

Shows emphasis.

我才不信他说的呢！

这才像个运动员的样子！

二、就

1．表示动作发生的时间早或迅速发生。

Expresses that something happened early or speedily.

他一醒来，天就亮了。

两岁时，他就成了孤儿。

你先等一会儿，他马上就来。

2．表示范围，相当于"只"。

Shows scope (similar to 只).

你以为就你一个人知道？

我就见过他一面。

他就会说。

3．和连词"只要、如果、既然"等连用。

Used with other conjunctions like 只要，如果，既然，etc.

只要你努力，就一定能学会。

如果他来了，你就告诉他。

既然学过，就不必再学了。

4. 表示同意。

Expresses agreement.

你要去那就去吧！

你不同意那就算了。

5. “才”和“就”连用。

才 and 就 used together.

(1) 后一件事紧接着前一件事发生。

The occurrence of a second thing happens immediately after the first.

他才说了两句话，你就打断了。

他才出去了一会儿，你就来了。

(2) 表示对比。

Shows comparison.

我学了半年才学会开车，他学了几个星期就学会了。

第九节 还、更

一、还

1. 表示行为、动作、性状不变。

Shows that there is no change in behavior, action, or characteristics.

他还住在原来的地方。

他还是那么年轻。

2. 表示补充、扩大原来的范围。

Shows addition or extension of the original scope.

除了工作以外，他还学点外语。

他家新盖了房子，还买了拖拉机。

3. 表示程度高(限于用在“比”字句)。

Indicates a high degree (used only with 比).

小王比他还高。

他比我还怕冷。

4. 表示程度不高。

Indicates a low degree.

这间屋子还干净。

他人还可以。

5. 相当于“只”“仅仅”。

Similar to 只，仅仅.

他还是个孩子。

今年还剩下没几天了。

6. 表示让步，相当于“尚且”。

Concessionary, similar to 尚且.

你还是大学生呢，连这点道理也不懂。

走还不会呢，就想跑？

二、更

“更”是程度副词。

更 is an adverb of degree.

1. 用在比较句里，表示程度高。

Used in comparative sentences to show a high degree.

他比我更了解农村。

今年的生产比去年更好。

2. 表示强调。

Expresses emphasis.

对于一个作家来说，更重要的是了解人民群众的生活和思想。

更可笑的是他忘了自己说了什么。

练　习

一、选词填空：

还　又　更　也　都　才　就　再　不　没有　比

1. 这(　　)是为了你好，并没有别的意思。
2. (　　)十点了，你怎么(　　)不起床？
3. 现在不走，(　　)赶不上火车了。
4. 你已经来过中国了，这(　　)不是第一次。
5. 他就是这么一个人，什么(　　)不在乎。
6. 现在时间(　　)早，咱们(　　)等一会儿吧。
7. 几乎所有的人(　　)参加了昨天的纪念活动。
8. 他比过去显得(　　)年轻了。
9. 我(　　)不信你说的这些话呢！
10. 如果我(　　)忘记的话，你是去年秋天来的。

11. 我(　　)去是因为我(　　)想去。

12. 我是从来(　　)喝酒的。

13. 市民的购买力(　　)往年有大幅度的增加。

14. (　　)是因为你,我才放弃了旅行计划。

15. (　　)大的困难也不能动摇我们的决心。

16. 他的绘画水平比某些画家(　　)高。

二、辨词填空:

1. 牛郎的哥哥(　　)牛郎很不好。(对、对于)

2. (　　)举办下届奥林匹克运动会的地点已经确定了。(对于、关于)

3. 事情全(　　)他弄坏了。(把、被)

4. 房间都(　　)收拾好了。(被、给)

5. 他俩是经过别人介绍(　　)认识的。(就、才)

6. 从这里坐公共汽车半个小时(　　)到。(才、就)

7. 他(　　)比你聪明。(不、没有)

8. 他比去年(　　)胖了。(还、更)

9. 他走了一会儿(　　)回来了。(又、再)

10. 他问了一个问题(　　)一个问题。(又、再)

11. 只要你多练习,(　　)学(　　)会的。(不、没有)

12. 你要是(　　)想去,你就(　　)去。(不、没有)

13. 现在商店里没这种货,过几天(　　)来看看。(又、再)

14. 你已经看过了,怎么(　　)看?(又、再)

15. 你别看他年龄不大,什么他(　　)知道。(都、也)

16. 他是记者,同时(　　)是作家。(都、也)

三、指出下列各句中带点的词所表示的意义:

1. 冬天,树叶都落了。　　　　(　　　　　)

现在都十二月了。　　　　(　　　　　)

2. 这孩子挺聪明,就是有点淘气。　　　　(　　　　　)

他十五岁就考上了大学。 (　　　　　)

3. 还不到一年，那座楼就盖起来了。 (　　　　　)

三十年过去了，那座庙还是老样子。 (　　　　　)

4. 你再不来，大家就走了。 (　　　　　)

大家让他再唱一支歌。 (　　　　　)

5. 你没(有)理由不接受大家的批评。 (　　　　　)

他有三个星期没来看我了。 (　　　　　)

6. 火车五点才到，整整晚了一个钟头。 (　　　　　)

今天才星期三，不着急。 (　　　　　)

第七章　词　　序
Chapter Seven　Word Order

第一节　什么是词序
What Is Word Order?

人们说话是一句一句说的。每句话是由若干个词排列起来的，这若干个词的排列又是有次序的。这种排列次序在语法学上称作词序，也叫作语序。

People speak phrase by phrase. Each phrase is made up of a number of individual words and the arrangement of the words is in a certain order. In grammar this arrangement is called word order.

不同的语言，词序可能是不同的。汉语中的修饰语，无论是定语或是状语，一般只能放在中心语前面。这一点就不同于印欧语。

In different languages, the word order is different. In Chinese, qualifiers, whether they are attributives or adverbials, will generally appear before the head word. This is different from Indo-European languages.

在对外汉语教学中，我们从学生作业里的大量常见错误中发现，词序是学生学习汉语的一个难点，带有普遍性。请看下面的例句：

In teaching Chinese to foreigners, it is easy to see from the large number of errors in students' exercises that word order is a common problem for students studying Chinese. Let's look at the following sentences:

(1) * 我两个星期来中国了。

(2) * 他每天至少四次吃饭。

(3) * 他问我许多问题关于中国。

(4) * 祝英台不愿意结婚跟一个大官的儿子。

(5) * 也我的看法不一样。

(6) * 今天的天气不丝毫冷。

(7) * 数学对我很有兴趣。

(8) * 把书必须拿回来。

(9) * 我不知道什么时候能够回来中国。

(10) * 上海是一个中国最大的工业城市。

例(1)里的“两个星期”补充说明“来中国”的时间,只能放在宾语“中国”之后。例(2)里的“四次”说明动作“吃饭”的次数,应该放在“吃”和“饭”之间。例(3)里的“关于中国”是限制宾语“问题”的,因此要放在“问题”之前,“许多”之后。因为“关于中国”是介宾词组,不能直接作定语,作定语时后面需带上“的”。例(4)里的“跟一个大官的儿子”是介宾词组,指明“结婚”的对象,应该放在动词“结婚”之前作方式状语。例(5)中的“也”是副词,在句中作状语,应该放在主语“看法”之后,谓语“不一样”之前。例(6)中的副词“丝毫”,只能放在否定词“不”之前,表示“不冷”的程度。例(7)中是“我有兴趣”,不是“数学有兴趣”,因此“我”是主语,“对数学”是介宾词组作“很有兴趣”的状语。例(8)中的“必须”是助动词,位置应该放在“把”字前边。例(9)中“回来中国”应该是“回中国来”,动词带趋向补语,同时又带处所宾语,处所宾语只能放在动补结构之间。例(10)里的“一个”应该放在“中国最大的”之后,“工业城市”之前。定语的次序是表示领属性的词放在最前边,其次是带“的”词语,再次是数量结构,最后是直接修饰中心语的名词。

In the first sentence, 两个星期 provides the information regarding the time of 来中国, and it can only follow the object 中国. In sentence (2) 四次 tells the number of times of the action 吃饭 and should be placed between 吃 and 饭. 关于中国 in the third sentence limits the object 问题 and should precede 问题 and follow 许多. Because 关于中国 is a prepositional object phrase, it cannot directly serve as an attributive. To be an attributive, 的 must be added. In sentence (4) 跟一个大官的儿子 is a prepositional object phrase indicating the object of 结婚 and should be placed before the verb 结婚 to serve as an adverbial of mode. In sentence (5), 也 is an adverb serving as a sentence adverbial and should be placed after the subject 看法 and before the predicate 不一样. The adverb 丝毫 in sentence (6) can only be placed in front of the negative 不 to show the degree of 不冷. Sentence (7) should be 我有兴趣 not 数学有兴趣. This way 我 is the subject. 对数学 is a prepositional object phrase serving as adverbial for 很有兴趣. 必须 in sentence (8) is an auxiliary verb and ought to be placed before 把. In sentence (9) 回来中国 should be 回中国来. When a verb has a directional complement and an object of location, the object of location must come between the verb and the complement. In sentence (10), 一个 should come after 中国最大的 and before 工业城市. In order, an attributive expressing possession will come first, then a word taking 的; next, numeral measure word construction; last, a noun directly qualifying the head word.

第二节 词序变换

Changes in Word Order

词序是词组或句子内部词的排列次序。词序不同,词组或句子内部的结构也不同。汉语中的词序在一定条件下是可以变换的,变换之后,有些句子的意思变化不大,有些句子的意思变化很大。下面列举七种词序变换的形式:

Word order is the order of arrangement of words in phrases and sentences. When the word order is different, the internal structure of phrases and sentences is different. Under certain conditions, word order in Chinese can be changed. In some sentences this changes the meaning very little; in other cases the changes in meaning are significant. The following examples show seven ways to change word order:

一、主谓变换 Exchange subject and predicate

(1) 一斤苹果/八毛钱。
八毛钱/一斤苹果。

(2) 苹果/八毛钱一斤。
苹果/一斤八毛钱。

(3) 他什么都懂。
什么他都懂。

例(1)是主谓句中主谓之间的变换。例(2)是主谓谓语句中谓语里的主语和谓语之间的变换。例(1)和例(2)是不同句子结构里的主谓变换,由于各个成分完全相同,其基本意思也相同。不过,此种变换只限于数量词作谓语的情况(如市场上的报价)。例(3)也是主谓谓语句,其变换形式是大主语和谓语中的小主语的位置变换,主语由表示任指的疑问代词"什么"来充当。因此不能把它看成是"他都懂什么?"的变换式,后者的"什么"要求回答,表示具体实在的意义。

In the first example there is an exchange of subject and predicate in a subject-predicate sentence. In sentence (2) there is an exchange of subject and predicate in the predicate of a sentence with a subject-predicate predicate. Examples (1) and (2) are an exchange of subject and predicate in sentences with different structures. Because the units are equivalent, the basic meaning is still the same. However, this type of exchange is possible only when the predicate is a numeral measure word (as price quoting in the market). Example (3) is also a sentence with a subject-predicate predicate with the exchange of main subject with the subject in the predicate. The all inclusive interrogative pronoun 什么 fills in the subject slot. It cannot be changed to "他都懂什么?" because this 什么 coming at the end is requesting an answer, expressing the actual meaning.

二、主宾变换 Exchange of subject and object

(1) 花开了。
开花了。

(2) 北京到了。
到北京了。

(3) 我看过那本小说了。
那本小说我看过了。

(4) 客人来了。
来客人了。

例(1)(2)(3)变换之后不改变句子的基本意思。例(1)中的“花”出现在谓语前是主语,出现在动词“开”后是宾语。“花”既是“开”的主动者,又是“开”的结果。例(2)里的主语宾语“北京”都表示处所。例(3)中“那本小说”是动词“看”的宾语,又可以出现在主语位置上。例(4)变换之后语义有变化。“客人来了”中的“客人”是受事主语,是有定的,预先知道客人是谁,“来客人了”中的“客人”是无定的。

The changes in (1), (2) and (3) do not change the basic meanings. 花 in (1) which appears in front of the predicate is the subject; when it appears after the verb 开 it is the object. 花 is the activator of 开 and is also the result. In (2) both the subject and object 北京 shows location. In (3) 那本小说 is the object of the verb 看 and can also appear in the subject position. In sentence (4) there is some change in meaning after the change. 客人 in 客人来了 is a patient subject and is definite. It is known beforehand who the guests are. 客人 in 来客人了 is indefinite.

三、“主动宾”句—“把”字句—“被”字句 The S-V-O sentence—The 把 sentence—The 被 sentence

传统语法学家认为“把”字句和“被”字句都是从“主动宾”句变来的。根据是“把”字的宾语在语义上是后边动词的受事,“被”字的宾语在语义上是后边动词的施事;前者“把”字提前了宾语,后者“被”字引出施事者。另一种看法认为“把”字的作用在于表示处置，强调主语的主动性；“被”字的作用在于表示遭受，强调主语的被动性。第三种看法认为“把”字句是由“把＋受事主语句”构成的，“被”字句是一种带“被”字的受事主语句。

虽然各家对“把”字句、“被”字句的看法不同，可是都不否认“把”字句、“被”字句和“主动宾”句之间存在着变换关系。请看例句：

Traditional grammarians believed that 把 and 被 sentences were transformations of S-V-O sentences. The basis for this was that the object of 把 is the semantic patient of the verb which follows, while the object of 被 is the semantic agent of the verb which follows. 把 preposed the object while 被 pointed out the agent. Another opinion is that 把 indicates management(disposal) and emphasizes the initiative of the subject. The function of 被 is to express being subjected to something and emphasize the passivity of the subject. A third theory holds that 把 sentence is constructed from 把 + a patient-subject sentence. 被 sentence is a kind of patient-subject sentence with a 被.

Although the opinions of scholars differ about 把 and 被 sentences, no one denies that there is a transformational relationship between 把 sentence, 被 sentence and the S-V-O sentence. Let's look at the examples:

(1)
- 猫吃鱼了。
- 猫把鱼吃了。
- 鱼被猫吃了。

(2)
- 雨淋棉花了。
- 雨把棉花淋了。
- 棉花被雨淋了。

(3) 我浇花了。
我把花浇了。
*花被我浇了。(花被我浇死了。)

(4) 他问得我张口结舌。
他把我问得张口结舌。
我被他问得张口结舌。

以上例句说明"把"字句、"被"字句和"主动宾"句存在着变换关系。但是,"把"字句和"被"字句有着很大不同。

首先,能出现在"把"字句和"被"字句里的及物动词是有限的,动词成分是个复杂形式。

The above examples show that there is a transformational relationship between 把 sentence,被 sentence and S-V-O sentence. But 把 sentence and 被 sentence are different in many ways.

First, the transitive verbs which can appear with 把 and 被 are limited. The verb element must be a complex form.

其次,"把"字的宾语一定在句中出现。"被"字的宾语不一定出现,如"被偷、被困、被抢、被杀、被击败"等。可见,"被"的作用不仅在于介绍出施事者,还在于表示被动。

Second, the object of 把 must appear in the sentence; the object of 被 does not have to appear. For example:被偷,被困,被抢,被杀,被击败,etc.

Clearly the function of 被 is not only to introduce the agent but also to express passivity.

第三,否定"把"字提前宾语的理由是有的"把"字句不能还原为"主动宾"句,因为这类"把"字句里动词后边另有宾语或其他成分。

Third, the reason to argue against 把 preposing an object is that some 把 sentences cannot be changed back to an S-V-O sentences, because this type of 把 sentence has an additional object or other element.

他把画挂在墙上。

把时间比作金子。

有些"把"字句是可以还原为"主动宾"句的。

Some 把 sentences can be change to S-V-O form.

你把信发了。

我把屋子收拾收拾。

你要把问题搞清楚。

他把字典还我了。

第四,"被"字句是一种受事主语句,可是有的受事主语句不能变成"被"字句。

Fourth, 被 sentence is a kind of patient-subject sentence, but patient-subject sentences cannot be changed to 被 sentences.

字被我写完了。

花被我浇过了。

用了"被"字反而显得很别扭。如果我们把意思稍加补充,变成"字被我写坏了""花被我浇死了",句子就可以说了。这是因为动词带上了不企望、不如意的结果补语。可是像"他被选为代表""他被评为先进"表示的并非不如意的事,也可以说。不过这种句子不多,而且主语和宾语等同,无法还原为"主动宾"句。

Using 被 makes the sentence awkward. If we alter the meaning slightly (字被我写坏了,花被我浇死了), the sentences are OK. This is because the verb has a complement showing negative expectation or undesirable result. However, sentences such as 他被选为代表,他被评为先进 do not show undesirable things, but can be used. This type of sentence is rare, and since the subject and the object represent the same thing, there is no way to change them to a S-V-O sentence.

四、状语的位置变换 Changes in position of adverbials

这里主要指的是副词作状语的情况。

We are primarily concerned with adverbs serving as adverbials.

(1) 电灯忽然灭了。
忽然电灯灭了。

(2) 他也许不知道。
也许他不知道。

(3) 他迟早会回来的。
迟早他会回来的。

在三组例句中,由于"忽然""也许""迟早"出现的位置不同,整个句子的结构关系也改变了。每组里的前一个句子是主谓结构,后一个句子是偏正结构。类似可前可后变换的双音节副词还有"毕竟、不妨、不过、迟早、处处、从此、大概、单单、当然、到底、的确、顿时、反正、仿佛、果然、何尝、忽然、居然、恐怕、明明、难道、偏偏、起初、起码、轻易、恰巧、是否、万一、无非、未必、幸亏、一时、终究、终于"等。不过,有的像"单单""偏偏"放在主语前后,意思并不完全相同。而绝大部分单音节副词只能放在主语后动词前作状语。

In the three groups of examples, when the positions of 忽然, 也许, and 迟早 are different, the structural relationships of the whole sentence are changed. In each group, the first sentence is a subject-predicate construction; the second is an endocentric construction. Other similar disyllabic adverbs which can be placed before or after are 毕竟,不妨,不过,迟早,处处,从此,大概,单单,当然,到底,的确,顿时,反正,仿佛,果然,何尝,忽然,居然,恐怕,明明,难道,偏偏,起初,起码,轻易,恰巧,是否,万一,无非,未必,幸亏,一时,终究,终于 etc.

However, a few such as 单单,偏偏 will have somewhat different meaning depending on whether they are placed before or after the subject. Most of the monosyllabic adverbs serving as adverbial can only be put after the subject and before the verb.

五、"在+名+动"和"动+在+名"的变换 Changing "在+noun+verb" to "verb+在+noun"

由介词"在"组成的介宾词组可以放在动词前也可以放在动词后。

Prepositional phrases formed with 在 and an object may be placed either before or after a verb.

(1) 他在城里住。
他住在城里。

(2) 钟在墙上挂着。
钟挂在墙上。

(3) 他在饭店门口站着。
他站在饭店门口。

在三组例句中,"在城里""在墙上""在饭店门口"都是指明事物以某种状态存在的处所。如果动作是具体的行为动作,那么动作的处所只能放在动词前边,不能放在动词后边。例如:

In the three examples 在城里,在墙上,在饭店门口 all point out a place in which something was existing in a specific state. If the action is a specific, concrete behavior, then the location of the action can be placed only in front of the verb, not following the verb. For example:

(4) { 他在公园里照相。
      * 他照相在公园里。

(5) { 他在湖里游泳。
      * 他游泳在湖里。

如果动词所表示的意义是抽象的，那么表示动作处所的词语只能放在动词之后，不能放在动词之前。例如：

If the meaning of the verb is abstract, then the language expressing the location of action can be placed only after the verb; it cannot precede the verb.

(6) { 你就看在朋友的面上吧。
      * 你就在朋友的面上看吧。

(7) { 他永远活在人们心里。
      * 他永远在人们心里活。

六、双宾语位置的变换 Position changes of double objects

汉语动词里有少数可以直接带双宾语，如果和"给"连用，双宾语的位置变换十分自由。例如：

A few verbs in Chinese may take two objects. If used with 给, the position of the double objects may be changed quite freely. For example:

(1) { 送(给)他几本书。
      送几本书给他。
      给他送几本书。

(2) 寄(给)他点钱。
寄点钱给他。
给他寄点钱。

(3) 借(给)他把钳子。
借把钳子给他。
给他借把钳子。

这类动词还有“发、找、递、分、退、租、夹、还”等。

Other such verbs are 发,找,递,分,退,租,夹,还,etc.

七、复谓式变换 Position changes of double predicates

连谓句中有一类前一个动作表示的是后一个动作的方式,这一类连谓句的两个动词结构可以变换其位置。例如:

There is one type of linked-predicate sentence in which what is expressed in the first action is the way or manner in which the second action is done. With this type of sentence, the position of the two verbal units may be changed.

(1) 他骑车上班。
他上班骑车。

(2) 他提着篮子买菜。
他买菜提着篮子。

(3) 他开着窗户睡觉。
他睡觉开着窗户。

(4) 他昧着良心说话。
他说话昧着良心。

变换后的句子表示的是经常性的习惯性的动作方式,带有某种修辞色彩。

有些连谓句虽然前一个动作表示方式，但是不能变换其位置，或者变换之后意义发生了变化。例如：

What is expressed in the sentences after the change is the usual habitual manner of the action; there is a certain rhetorical tone.

With some linked predicates, although the first action expresses manner, the positions may not be changed or the result will be a changed in meaning.
For example:

(1) 他睁着眼睛说瞎话。
  *他说瞎话睁着眼睛。

(2) 他捂着耳朵装听不见。
  *他装听不见捂着耳朵。

(3) 他蒙着头大睡。
  *他大睡蒙着头。

(4) 他坐飞机去上海。
  他去上海坐飞机。

(5) 他打电话通知我。
  他通知我打电话。

前三组里的第二句都不能说，因为表示的不是经常性的、习惯性的动作。后两组里的第二句与第一句意义有别。第四组里"他去上海坐飞机"的意思是他去上海后改乘飞机。第五组里"他通知我打电话"，其结构关系已变为递系结构，意思是他通知我，我去打电话。

由"让"组成的递系结构里，否定词"别"的位置可前可后，但意义和语气有区别。例如：

With the first three groups, the second sentence is unacceptable, because what is expressed is not a usual, habitual action. With the last two groups, the second sentence produces a different meaning.

In the fourth group, 他去上海坐飞机 means that after getting to Shanghai he got on a plane. In the fifth group 他通知我打电话, the structure has become a ranked structure meaning "he notified me and I made a phone call".

In ranked structures using 让, the position of the negative 别 may be before or after. But there is a difference in meaning and tone. For example:

(1) 你让他别去。
你别让他去。

(2) 你让他别生气。
你别让他生气。

例(1)中前者有说服劝阻之意,后者有阻拦、制止之意。例(2)中前者是你劝他别生气,后者是你别再使他生气。

In the first group, 你让他别去 implies persuading or advising. 你别让他去 indicates prevention or stopping. In the second group, the first sentence means you should exhort him not to be angry. The second means you should not make him angry.

词序是句子结构的外部形式特征,它是受语义结构关系制约的。词序变换也是在语义结构关系不变的条件下进行的,它反映了汉语表达形式多样性的特点。由于汉语里的词组和句子的构造原则是一致的,因此,词序基本上是稳定的,有规律可循的。

Word order is a feature of the external form of sentence structure. It is influenced by restrictions of semantic relationships. Rearranging word order is also carried out under the condition that semantic relationships are not affected. This illustrates that Chinese has many different forms of expression. Because the principles of structure are the same for phrases and for sentences in Chinese, word order is essentially stable, with rules which can be followed.

练　　习

一、指出下列各组句子中正确的句子：

1. 我想济南比泰山没有意思。 (　)
2. 我想济南不比泰山有意思。 (　)
3. 我想济南没有泰山有意思。 (　)

1. 他喝了一杯又一杯。 (　)
2. 他喝了一杯再一杯。 (　)
3. 他喝了一杯还一杯。 (　)

1. 不去过沙漠的人不知道水的宝贵。 (　)
2. 没去过沙漠的人没知道水的宝贵。 (　)
3. 没去过沙漠的人不知道水的宝贵。 (　)

1. 将来有机会我想还到这儿来。 (　)
2. 将来有机会我还想到这儿来。 (　)
3. 将来有机会我再想到这儿来。 (　)

1. 他才说了一句，你就打断了。 (　)
2. 他就说了一句，你才打断了。 (　)
3. 他才说了一句，你才打断了。 (　)

二、仿例写出下列句子的变换式：

在银行里存钱——→钱存在银行里——→银行里存着钱

在合同上签字

在信封上贴邮票

在背心上印字

在地板上打蜡

在葫芦里装药
在冰箱里放肉
在沙漠里打井
在宇宙里航行
在面包里夹黄油
在阳台上晒太阳
在森林里过夜
在冰场上滑冰
在站台上接人
在法庭上作证
在深山里采药
在朋友家里作客

三、仿例写出下列句子的变换式：

他比我年轻——→我不如他年轻——→我没有他年轻
他比我聪明
他比我学得好
他比过去胖
他来得比我早
夏天比冬天舒服
城里比城外热闹
昨天比今天冷
滑冰比打球有意思
他比我能唱
光速比声速快
工业比农业发展快
晴天比阴天多
坐车比骑车快
他比我了解

他比我运气好
时间比金子宝贵

第八章　现代汉语语法的特点
Chapter Eight　Special Features of Modern Chinese Grammar

一、缺少严格意义上的形态变化　Lacking morphological change in the strict sense

形态标志(morphological marker)在印欧语中是很丰富的。名词、形容词有性、数、格的变化，动词有人称、时态的变化。英语里，名词复数用"s"表示：book—books(书)。动词一般现在时、单数第三人称用"s"表示：He works in the factory.(他在工厂工作。)定冠词 the 用来表示确定的说话双方都知道的人或事物：Where is the book?(书在哪儿?)

Indo-European languages have many morphological signs. Nouns and adjectives have form changes for gender, number, and case. Verbs change for person and tense. For example in English, "s" is added to show plural: book - books. A verb in its present tense and singular third person uses "s": He works in the factory. "The" is used to show definite person or thing that both the speaker and the listener know about: Where is the book?

汉语里究竟有没有形态或形态变化？许多语言学家做了大量

的研究,基本上确认汉语里没有形态变化,或者说缺少严格意义上的形态标志。

有些词看上去类似形态标志,但是不明显。如"了""着""过"总是跟在动词之后,表示某种时态。

Does Chinese have morphology or morphological changes? Many linguists have engaged in extensive research and have determined that Chinese has no morphological change. In other words, in the strictest sense of the word, it lacks morphological signs.

Some words seem to have a similarity to morphological signs, but it is not obvious. For example: 了,着 and 过 always follow verbs to express some kind of tense.

我写了一封信。 (表示完成 expresses completion)

窗户开着。 (表示持续 expresses continuation)

我看过这部电影。 (表示经历 expresses experience)

有的人便把"了""着""过"看作动词后缀(suffix)。可是,"了""过"既可以附在动词后边,又可以附在动补结构之后(如"写完了信""昨天他回来过")。"着"只能附在动词后边,不能附在动词结构之后(如不能说"写完着信");有时能附在动词"有"之后,但并不表示时态(如"他有着惊人的记忆力")。可见,把它们看作形态标志是有困难的。

Some scholars consider 了,着, and 过 as verb suffixes. But 了 and 过 may be added after verb or at the end of a verb-complement structure (写完了信,昨天他回来过). 着 may be added only after the verb, not after a verb-complement structure(写完着信 ×). When 着 follows the verb 有, it does not express tense (他有着惊人的记忆力). It is clear that calling them morphological signs presents difficulties.

二、汉语句子的构造原则跟词组的构造原则是一致的

The Principles of structure are the same for phrases and for sentences in Chinese

句子和词组都是句法结构存在的具体形式。汉语的基本句法结构形式有五种,即偏正结构、述宾结构、述补结构、主谓结构和联合结构。当这些句法结构处于单说时,它就是句子。当它出现在某个句子中,它便是词组。换句话说,就是句子的句法结构和词组的句法结构是完全一样的。例如:

Sentences and phrases are both concrete forms of syntactic structure. There are 5 basic types of syntactic structure in Chinese: endocentric, verb-object, verb-complement, subject-predicate, and compound. When such syntactic structure are used alone, they are sentences; when they appear within a sentence, they are phrases. In other words, the syntactic structure of sentences and phrases is exactly the same. For example:

	句子	词组
偏正结构:	很好。	(天气)很好
述宾结构:	坐火车。	坐火车(太慢)
述补结构:	写清楚。	(信)写清楚
主谓结构:	他去。	他去(最好)
联合结构:	聪明大方。	(她)聪明大方

可见,无论单说还是出现在句子里边,它们的句法结构都不改变。

在印欧语里,句子的构造跟词组的构造不同。在英语里,句子的谓语动词必须是限定形式,而在词组里,只能是不定式或者是分词形式,不能用限定形式。例如:

Whether used alone or within a sentence, their syntactic structure does not change.

In Indo-European languages, sentence structure and the structure of phrases are not the same. For example, in English the verb in the predicate must be a finite form, but in a phrase it must be an infinitive or a participle. For example:

He reads the book.（他读那本书。）

The book is easy to read.（那本书很容易读。）

Reading the book is easy.（读那本书很容易。）

在头一句里，谓语动词 reads 是限定形式，在后两句里 to read 是不定式，reading 是分词形式。

汉语里的动词或动词结构无论出现在哪里，形式完全一样。

In the first sentence, the predicate verb "reads" is in finite form; in the last two sentences "to read" is an infinitive, "reading" is a participle.

In Chinese, no matter where a verb or verb construction appears, the form is the same.

三、主谓结构可以作谓语 Subject-predicate structure can act as predicate

主谓谓语句是汉语里比较常见的重要句式。例如：

In Chinese, the subject-predicate predicative sentence is a frequent and important sentence form. For example:

他学习很努力。

语法他没学过。

明天我们进城。

北京公园很多。

花生两块一斤。

这些句子在结构上的一个共同特点是整个句子是由主语和谓语两部分组成的，而谓语部分又是由主谓结构组成的。从语义上看，第一句和第四句里的大主语和小主语（指谓语里的主语）之间有一种领属关系。然而，我们不能因此把“他学习”看作“他的学习”，把“北京公园”看作“北京的公园”，因为在大小主语之间可以有停顿，而且还可以插入其他成分。如：“他一向学习很努力。”“北京现在公园很多。”这正是主语和谓语之间才具有的特点。第二句里的主语“语法”在意义上是后边动词“学”的受事。但是，我们不能把它看作是“宾语提前”，因为，“主—动—宾”式是汉语的基本句式。主语在前，谓语在后是汉语句式的特点，主语和宾语之间没有直接的关系。主语不一定只限于施事者，也可以是受事者；宾语不一定只限于受事者，也可以是施事者。如：“来客人了。”如果把这句看成主语后置，便把语义和结构混为一谈了。第三句里的“明天”和第五句里的“花生”，我们不妨把它们看作是话题，从句子表达功能上看是完全讲得通的。我们不能因为“明天”表示时间，就取消了它作主语的资格。

The structural feature shared by all of these sentences is that they are composed of two parts: subject and predicate; furthermore, the predicate is also a subject predicate construction. In terms of semantics, in the first and fouth sentences, the main subject and the second subject (the subject in the predicate) have a kind of possessive relationship. However, we cannot look upon 他学习 as 他的学习 or 北京公园 as 北京的公园 because there can be a pause between the main subject and the second subject. In addition, other element may be inserted, as 他一向学习很努力, 北京现在公园很多. This is indeed a unique feature between subject and predicate.

The subject 语法 in the second sentence is the semantic patient of the verb which follows. But we must not consider this as a preposed object. S-V-O is the basic sentence form in Chinese. Subject first, predicate second is a characteristic of Chinese sentence form, and there is no direct relation between subject and object. The subject is not limited to the agent but can also be the patient. The object is not limited to the patient, but can also be the agent. As in 来客人了. If the sentence is considered as subject being placed last, then it is confusing semantics and structure. There is nothing against viewing 明天 in the third sentence and 花生 in the fifth as topics. From the expressive function of the sentence this is entirely possible. We cannot eliminate 明天 as a possible subject simply because it expresses time.

四、有丰富的虚词系统 Having a complete system of function words

由于汉语缺少形态变化,因此,虚词在汉语语法中占有十分重要的地位。可以说,虚词是组成句子结构不可缺少的材料。

Because there are no morphological change in Chinese, function words hold a very important position in Chinese grammar. In fact, function words are essential material for forming sentence structures.

虚词的特点 Characteristics of function words:

1. 表示语法意义 Expressing grammatical meaning

如"很"表示程度,"的"表示领属,"了"表示动作的完成,"把"表示处置,"被"表示被动,"吧"表示语气。

很 indicates degree, 的 shows possession, 了 implies the completion of an action, 把 shows disposal, 被 expresses passiveness, and 吧 shows some tone.

2. 位置固定 Position is fixed.

虚词一般不能单说,它总是附在某个实词的前后,活动能力受限制(少数除外,如"也许""大概""未必")。如"了""着""过"往往出现在动词后面,"吧""吗""呢"一般出现在句子的末尾,副词常常出现在动词、形容词前面。

Most function words cannot be used alone (with only a few exceptions:也许,大概,未必). They are always added before or after certain notional words. Their ability to move is limited. For example:

了,着,and 过 usually appear after verbs.

吧,吗,and 呢 generally appear at the end of a sentence.

Adverbs often appear before verbs and adjectives.

3. 使用频率高 Used frequently.

虚词大约有七百个,比实词要少得多。常用虚词二百个左右,可是出现频率相当高。据统计数字表明,"的"是出现频率最高的。其次像"了""很""也""还""就""都"等也是使用频率相当高的。

There are about 700 function words, not nearly as many as there are notional words. There are about 200 commonly used function words, but the rate of appearance or use is very high. Statistical counts show that 的 appears most frequently. Those next in frequency such as 了,很,也,还,就,都 far surpass the use of notional words.

虚词数量尽管少,而且一般只表示语法意义,可是在语法系统里,虚词却有一套严密的分工系统。以副词为例:

Although their numbers are small and usually they express only grammatical meaning, function words nevertheless have a very tight system of division of labor.

Take adverbs for example:

程度副词:很、大、更、最、十分、非常

范围副词:都、也、只、单单、仅仅

时间副词:正、刚、才、就、还、先、再

否定副词:不、没(有)、未、别

语气副词:偏(偏)、倒、究竟、简直、未免

数量副词:正好、刚好、才、只、都

方式副词:一直、亲手、互相、只好、特地

五、有丰富的量词 Having a complete set of measure words

量词表示事物的单位。事物有具体和抽象之分,量词没有这个区别。如"个"既可用来指人和物,又可指抽象的事物。

Measure word is the unit of things, regardless of concret or abstract things. 个 can be used with people and concret things as well as with abstract things.

个 { 一个人 一个西瓜
一个问题 一个机会

有的量词用于不同的名词。例如:

Certain measure words are used with different nouns. For example:

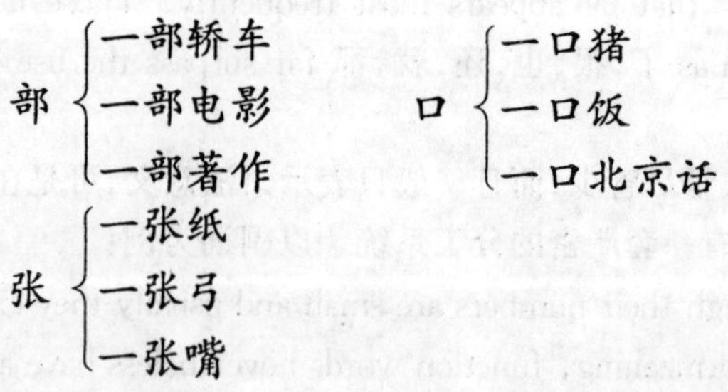

有的名词不只一个量词。例如:

Some nouns can take more than one measure word. For example:

鱼 { 一条鱼 / 一尾鱼 }　药 { 一片药 / 一剂药 / 一丸药 }

量词分名量词和动量词,名量词和动量词又分专用和借用两类。

Measure words are divided into nominal measure words and verbal measure words. Nominal and verbal measure words are further divided into specialized measure words and borrowed measure words.

- 量词
  - 名量词
    - 专用量词:个、张、把、条、只、双、对、套
    - 借用量词:车、箱子、碗、瓶、里
  - 动量词
    - 专用量词:次、下、回、遍、场
    - 借用量词:(看)一眼、(喝)一口
(说)一说、(想)一想

第九章　常见语法错误分析

Chapter Nine　Analysis of Common Grammatical Errors

在学习一种语言的过程中，由于人们对词的意义和用法理解掌握得不准确、不全面，对句子结构缺乏认识，常常会出现语法错误。这些错误归纳起来大致有以下几种。

In the course of studying a language, many grammatical errors occur either because the understanding of the meaning and use of words is inaccurate and incomplete or because there is a lack of the knowledge of syntactic structure. These errors can be summarized in the following kinds:

一、成分残缺　Missing elements

成分残缺是指句子里缺少了必不可少的成分。例如：

A sentence lacks an essential part which cannot be omitted. For example:

(1) 从我懂事的时候起，便和大海交上了朋友。

(2) 当他毕业时，已经二十八岁了。

(3) 听到他的歌声,使我想起童年的生活。

(4) 中国人真有智慧的民族。

(5) 你真革命性的人物啊!

(6) 他的小说反映了旧北京的市民。

例(1)(2)(3)缺主语,例(4)(5)缺谓语,(6)缺宾语。

(1),(2) and (3) lack subjects; (4) and (5) lack predicates; (6) lacks an object.

二、用词不当 Words used inappropriately

用词不当多数来自对词义理解错误或者是词性搞颠倒。例如:

Usually the word is not understood correctly or the syntactic function is reversed. For example:

(1) 他对中国的社会很精通。

(2) 北京大学在颐和园周围。

(3) 鲁班是中国古老的工匠。

(4) 植物园里的花显得很生动。

(5) 我朋友接受了一封信。

(6) 万一你到美国去,我就欢迎你。

(7) 妹妹年纪虽小,却很智慧。

(8) 这件事在我脑子里印象得很深。

前六句里的"精通""周围""古老""生动""接受""万一"都用得不合适,应改为"了解""附近""古代""美丽""收到""如果"。后两句里的"智慧""印象"都是名词,不能作形容词和动词来用,应改为"聪明""印"。

In the first six sentences,精通,周围,古老,生动,接受 and 万

一 are not properly used. They should be changed to 了解,附近,古代,美丽,收到,如果. In the last two sentences,智慧 and 印象 are nouns,and can't be used as adjective and verb. They should be corrected as 聪明 and 印 .

三、搭配不当 Inappropriate matching

搭配不当指成分之间在意义上不相干。例如:

The elements are not related in meaning. For example:

(1) 秋天的北京是金色的季节。

(2) 教室里的光线和空气非常流通。

(3) 山西的煤是我国最丰富的地区之一。

(4) 一九九二年我国工业增长的速度是最快的一年。

(5) 他已经掌握了医疗技术水平。

(6) 在改革中,这些人扮演了骨干作用。

上面六句中,"北京"和"季节"、"光线"和"流通"、"煤"和"地区"、"速度"和"年"、"掌握"和"水平"、"扮演"和"作用"在意义上没有联系。

In the above six sentences,北京 and 季节,光线 and 流通,煤 and 地区,速度 and 年,掌握 and 水平,扮演 and 作用 have no connection in meaning.

四、位置不当 Incorrect position

位置不当是指词的排列次序有错误。例如:

The order and arrangement of the words are incorrect. For

example:

(1) 早晨脑子是最清醒的时候。

(2) 数学对我很有兴趣。

(3) 开学已经三个月过去了。

(4) 今年夏天好几次下雨了。

(5) 每个奥地利人有在美国住的亲戚。

(6) 他讲了许多工厂里的新鲜事。

例(1)"是"应放在"脑子"前边。例(2)"数学"和"我"互换位置。例(3)"三个月"应放在"过去"后边。例(4)"好几次下雨了"应改为"下了好几次雨"。例(5)"有在美国住的亲戚"应改为"有亲戚住在美国"。例(6)"许多"应放在"工厂里的"后边。

In sentence (1),是 should precede 脑子. In sentence (2),数学 and 我 should replace each other. In sentence (3),三个月 should be put after 后边. In sentence (4),好几次下雨了 should be 下了好几次雨. In sentence (5),有在美国住在亲戚 should be 有亲戚住在美国. In sentence (6),许多 should follow 工厂里的 .

四、成分多余 Redundant element

句子里有了多余的成分,引起意思上的混乱。例如:

Because there are redundant elements in the sentence the meaning is unclear.

For example:

(1) 这项工程基本上全部完成了。

(2) 老年人对青年人的看法也改变了态度。

(3) 他不再怀疑黄鼠狼不吃鸡了。

(4) 那鲜艳的花朵,实在令人可爱。

(5) 他被挨了一顿骂。

(6) 我们用的是筷子吃饭的。

例(1)用了"基本上"不能再用"全部"。例(2)是"看法"改变了,后边不再用"态度"。例(3)"怀疑"吃鸡而不是"不吃鸡"。例(4)用了"可爱"不能再用"令人"。例(5)"挨"本身有被动的意思,再用"被"多余。例(6)改为"我们是用筷子吃饭的",句子简洁而明白。

In sentence (1),基本上 and 全部 conflict with each other. In sentence (2),what is changed is 看法,so 态度 should not be used. In sentence (3),what is doubted is 吃鸡,not 不吃鸡. In sentence (4),可爱 can't be used together with 令人. In sentence (5),挨 and 被 both indicate passiveness, so 被 is redundant. Sentence (6), will be more concise after being changed to 我们是用筷子吃饭的.

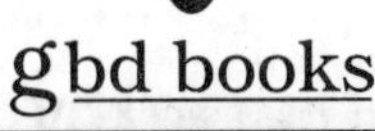

Rs. 180/-

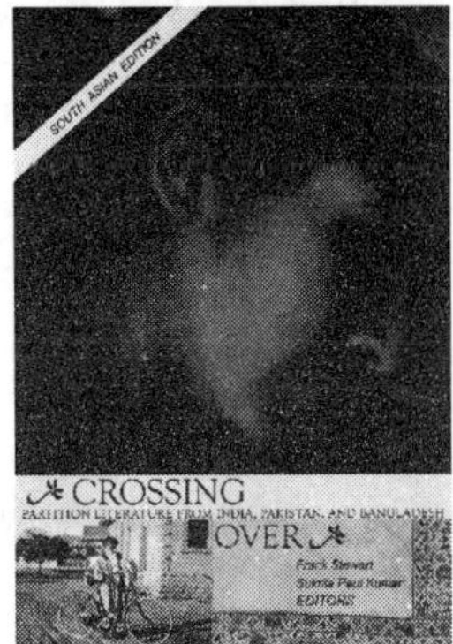

Rs. 295/-

Motivational Books by Richard Carswell

Rs. 295/- each

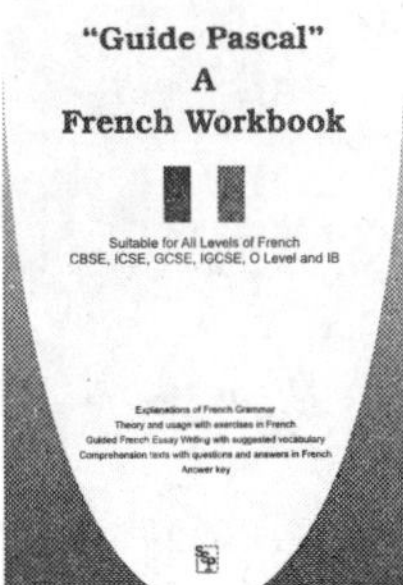

Rs. 195/-

Rs. 295/-

Rs. 125/-